THE PENGUIN BOOK OF
POLITICAL
COMICS

Steef Davidson was born in Amsterdam in 1943. He has been a runaway, a college drop-out and a visual artist. In the mid-sixties he became involved in the Provo movement and later edited and published the Dutch underground magazine *OM*. Since 1968 he has had seven books published in Holland and Germany on topics as varied as North American Indians, radical culture and comics. Among his other activities, he organizes exhibitions and writes poetry. He has worked on a brief history of Dutch–Indian relations in North America in the seventeenth century and an international anthology of political posters.

STEEF DAVIDSON

THE PENGUIN BOOK OF POLITICAL COMICS

TRANSLATED BY HESTER AND MARIANNE VELMANS

Penguin Books Ltd, Harmondsworth, Middlesex, England
Penguin Books, 625 Madison Avenue, New York, New York 10022, U.S.A.
Penguin Books Australia Ltd, Ringwood, Victoria, Australia
Penguin Books Canada Ltd, 2801 John Street, Markham, Ontario, Canada L3R 1B4
Penguin Books (N.Z.) Ltd, 182-190 Wairau Road, Auckland 10, New Zealand

Beelden Storm: De Ontwikkeling van de Politieke Strip first published by Van Gennep,
Amsterdam, 1976
Published in Penguin Books 1982

Made and printed in Great Britain by
William Clowes (Beccles) Ltd, Beccles and London

CONTENTS

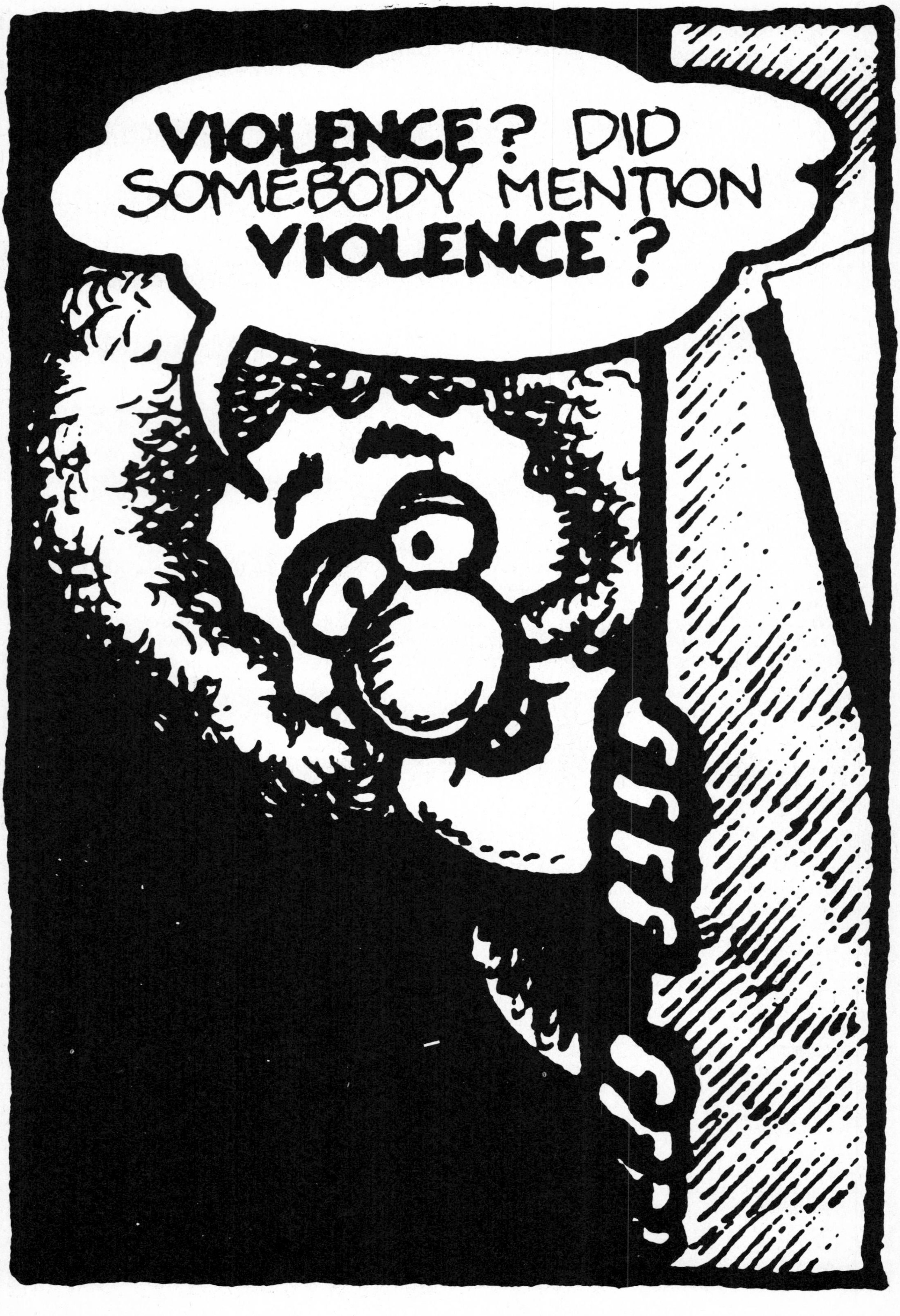
VIOLENCE? DID SOMEBODY MENTION VIOLENCE?

WARNING!

THIS IS PROPAGANDA

This book is about cartoon strips — and about political propaganda. Propaganda is the means by which a particular ideology is brought to life and comic strips are an ideal medium for the spreading of ideas and propaganda. Words or pictures on their own lack the direct impact of the two put together and illustrations will make the most theoretical text easier to understand.

In other comic strip anthologies, emphasis is put on the artist himself, and the main criterion is how famous he is. Here you will meet few famous names, because I want to present strips which are representative of the grass-roots movements from which they originated.

Whether they are meant to be educational or whether they are intended for pure entertainment, all comic strips contain a certain measure of political bias or opinion, even if it is only a caricatured one. Cartoonists can't help reflecting the moral, political and cultural climate of their time. Look at W.K. Haselden's strip for example: today we can see it as a vicious piece of anti-communist propaganda, yet he was only reflecting the popular opinion of his time. It is easy to laugh at the naivety of such strips, or to become indignant at their racist, sexist or authoritarian overtones. However, I have deliberately limited myself, in collecting strips for this book, to the ones that have been consciously created as propaganda.

Anybody who gets the chance to peruse the literature of political parties or movements will have noticed that comic strips appear there more and more frequently. Compared with the political propaganda of the past, the visual impact of papers, handbills and pamphlets has become all-important. In this, the political press follows the general pattern of our visually oriented culture, which in turn reflects the social conditions under which we live. The purpose of propaganda is to translate the language of a given culture, which is the product of social conditions, into a weapon which can change these social conditions. Revolutions don't happen out of the blue. The ideas leading to such upheavals are in the air long before the crunch comes.

This book is full of such ideas. Ideas that are alive now.

THE LONG MARCH THROUGH THE STUDIOS

It is only fairly recently that the political comic strip has come into its own as a mature genre. This is why this book concentrates on the developments in political consciousness over the last fifteen years and the strips which grew out of them. Nevertheless I shall start with a short historical survey, if only to establish them briefly in context. Although strip-like illustrations were around as early as 1800 for consciously propagandist purposes, it was really the growth of the newspaper that made the comic strip popular. For years after the invention of the camera, newspapers were still unable to reproduce photographs. For that reason most newspapers used artists to illustrate current affairs, the children's corner or the family weekend supplement. Elaborately illustrated children's books were also very popular in the nineteenth century, and the end of the century saw the appearance of children's stories in strip form. But it was in America that the comic strip really got off the ground, when newspapers started printing them for light relief. This was the birth of the comic strip as we know it.

Weaned in the daily press and directed at first at children, the comic was soon to develop into a huge industry with an audience of millions. Soon every paper had its own strip, and comics moved from the weekly children's supplements to the editorial pages in daily instalments. The combination of simple plots and bold drawings was meant to be 'educational'. Disobedience and naughtiness were invariably punished. The moral climate of the day was reflected in the comic strips: the bourgeois code of ethics was never criticized — for the whole idea was to boost sales, not shrink them.

If protest was taboo in the establishment press, it was the first requisite for a cartoon published in the more radical papers — for instance, in the pamphlets of the Industrial Workers of the World (IWW). This organization was the champion of the poor and exploited, European immigrants mainly, who had arrived in America in search of a better life. Cartoons and comic strips were obviously the ideal medium for propaganda directed at this motley, multilingual bunch, few of whom had mastered the English language, let alone the art of reading. In these cartoons the social message came first before artistic merit, so 'Mr Block' never reached the heights of fame of 'The Yellow Kid' or 'The Katzenjammerkids'. Soon every political group that boasted a journal made a point of including some cartoons or comic strips in its pages — and not only in America.

The first really popular comic strips which could be seen as a protest against current ethical standards appeared in the so-called Tijuana Bibles, illicitly published in the 1930s. They were also called 'eight-pagers' because they were eight-page pamphlets which presented popular comic strip heroes like Popeye and public figures like Gandhi, misbehavin' in porno-graphic scenarios. Tijuana was of course notorious as a bed of sin just the other side of the Mexican border. In fact, the sex industry of this border town depended on the custom of illicit fun-seeking Americans. For in spite of its technical and scientific superiority, America was an underdeveloped nation as far as sex was concerned, deeply puritanical and repressed. This had resulted in strict censorship. And it was to that deep-seated prudery that the 'eightpagers' owed their success. Over a thousand titles of these 'Bibles' are known, and we can assume that hundreds of thousands of copies were printed. Directed at an audience, their controversial nature made them politically significant.

The 1930s witnessed the appearance of political comic

strips in several European election campaigns. In format and style, they still owed much to the children's prints which were so popular in the nineteenth century — the bilderbogen. In Holland and Germany, these strips were fashionable, especially among the Social Democrats. During the Spanish Civil War, the Republicans found comic strips very useful for propaganda, especially in view of the fact that there was such a high proportion of illiterates among the Spanish people. Strips were used to simplify social and economic problems, or to explain the importance of discipline.

Towards the end of the thirties, stacks of comics were being imported from the United States into Europe. This stopped, of course, when the Nazis took over. But the Germans were well aware of the significance of the comic strip as a medium, and they tried to woo the youth of occupied Holland by sponsoring strips. One of their attempts was called 'Flits the Alsatian and Bull the Dog' and was published by the Department of Information and the Arts. The satirical magazine 'De Gil' ('The Scream'), which had Nazi sympathies, was also busy publishing comic-strip supplements.

Immediately after the liberation, twenty or so comic strips were published in Holland alone dealing with the Nazi occupation. The front and back covers of one such comic book, by Ton van Tast, are reproduced here and show the kind of things people thought they had missed during the occupation, and what they expected to gain from liberation.

Meanwhile, there had been new developments in America. By the time the Tijuana Bibles had faded from the scene in the forties, the comic industry had shifted its attentions to a new phenomenon: the superhero. The comic strip had grown up bit by bit with its audience: no longer directed at the barely literate youngest, the new genre was aimed at the 8- to 13-year-olds, who craved adventure and suspense — and who had pocket money to pay for their own comics. Crime became the main topic, and the heroes were invariably detectives and supermen who lived in a fantasy world where they were called upon to defend property and the moral code. They came in all shapes and sizes, but carried the same message: Batman, the embodiment of the triumph of good over evil in the future; Prince Valiant, representing honour and conscience in the past; and Dick Tracey, the famous present-day sleuth.

Strong enough to go it alone, the comics industry had now separated itself from the newspapers and the market was flooded with scores of weekly comic magazines and animated films. They partly owed their success to the fact that they never sounded the least note of satire or parody, and steered clear of controversy in any form. The comic-strip characters were created to imitate and promote the bourgeois way of life. Few cartoonists managed to defy this unwritten code. The only exceptions were the most surrealist artists, like Winsor McCay ('Little Nemo') and George Herriman ('Krazy Kat').

With the introduction of the law and order theme, however, a little of the grim reality of life was allowed to break through the gay mask of fun. For the first time, there were allusions to the seamier side of life, and this comparatively new realism in comics allowed the more negative aspects of society to be examined.

One of the first publishers to get involved in this area was Harry Donenfeld. The first issue of his Detective Comics (DC) was published in March 1937. A travelling salesman, M.C. Gaines (who had had some experience in producing cartoons for the giant Procter & Gamble corporation amongst others), then offered Donenfeld a new comic-book character. It was Superman. In a very short space of time, Superman had become a youth idol, a superstar. The personification of the American ideal, he was the champion of freedom and democracy, pitting his superhuman strength against unspeakable villains always plotting to destroy the wealth and freedom of the free world. His double identity, as the journalist Clark Kent, allowed everyone to identify with him. He was the first of a new dynasty of superheroes: Captain Marvel, Wonder Woman, Captain America, to name but a few. Even as the comic-strip villains became more cunning and their crimes more terrible, so the heroes became more super-spectacular. Marvel Comics, which were launched after Detective Comics, specialized in characters who were, wherever possible, more surreal and weird than Superman and his pals.

For almost two years, although it was ravaging Europe, the Second World War was almost completely ignored in the American comic magazines. Then came Pearl Harbor, and patriotism was unleashed overnight among America's superheroes. Without exception they strode into battle on the side of the Allies to combat Fascism. Captain Marvel took on Dr Nazi single-handed, and Captain America slew a Nippon Dracula who fed himself on the blood of American soldiers. And so the superheroes won the war and the comic industry grew and grew.

Not to everyone's approval, however. The comics' growing popularity and their preoccupation with crime and violence was, in right-wing opinion, one of the causes of growing violence and juvenile delinquency. In 1950, Congress instituted an inquiry into the possible connection between comics and juvenile delinquency. But the inquiry didn't come to anything and the industry continued to expand — until its critics returned a few years later, and better equipped this time. Their main targets were the crime and superhero comics. Donald Duck and Mickey Mouse and their furry friends they left alone.

The keeper of that particular little zoo (which strangely resembled America itself), Walt Disney, played strict censor for the cartoonists in his stable. He was especially watchful for anything that might be construed as criticism of any aspect of American society. Not that there was no criticism of Disney's own output: but this came from a different, more progressive quarter.

Mr. Block
He Tries To Be a Union Scab

IF WE ALL BECAME BOLSHEVISTS. . . .

Life would be conducted at the point of the pistol, by everybody against everybody else.

Hergé, *Tintin in America*, **Belgium, 1947.** © Casterman.
1. 'Golly! Oil! A liquid fortune! And nobody around to grab it!' 'I always thought petrol came in cans...' 2. 'Hello, boy! Just sign on the dotted line! I offer you $5,000 for your oil well.' 3. 'How...how did you know? It barely started gushing ten minutes ago...' 'I've got a nose for it, old boy! An American businessman doesn't make mistakes!' 4. 'Don't listen to that idiot! Just sign here...$10,000 for that oil well!...' 5. 'Don't sign old chap! I'll give you $25,000!...' '50,000!...' '100,000!...' 6. 'Gentlemen, I'm terribly sorry, but this oil well isn't mine! It belongs to the Blackfoot Indians on this reservation!' 'Why didn't ya say so before?' 7. 'Here is $5,000! You have half an hour to get yourselves together and scram!...' 'Paleface must be crazy!...' 8. An hour later... 9. Two hours later... 10. Three hours later... 11. The next morning... 'Who is that asshole?' 'Hey, mister, dontcha know it's illegal to walk about town in fancy dress? And keep your ass out of the way of the traffic! Ya think you're in the Wild West or something?'

11

HOE ZE ERACHTER KWAM

VERKIEZINGSPRENT DER S.D.A.P. VERSJES VAN O.K. PRENTJES VAN A.H. *1929*

Nazi's Außenpolitik
Hier siehst Du Adolf heimlich kosen Mit unsern „Feinden", den Franzosen. Im Innern, bei der Preußenwahl, Ist er jedoch „streng national".

Nazi-Sozialismus
Den Arbeitslosen, die im Dalles, Verspricht der gute Adolf alles — Dafür zahlt schmunzelnd eine Rate Die Industrie für Wahlplakate.

Nazi's Ein-bürgerung
Der Adolf wurde als Gendarm; In seiner Uniform wird's warm; In Braunschweig als Regierungsrat Ward deutsch er erst und — Kandidat.

Nazi-Programm
Im dritten Reich wird uns beglücken Der Aufschwung aller Sargfabriken Denn Best in Boxheim hat beschlossen: Wer nicht pariert, wird gleich erschossen!

Nazi's Legalität
Legalität! Verfassungstreu'! So schwören täglich sie aufs neue. Was gilt ein Eid von diesen Schlingeln, Die „ganz legal" Berlin umzingeln!?

Das nationale Kapital
Der Junker, der sich ruiniert, Wird, wie die Industrie, saniert. Die Republik greift in die Kassen Und darf zum Dank sich — stürzen lassen.

Die Schablone
Wer kommt denn da? Der Pinsel ist Wahrhaftig noch der Kommunist. Je mehr der nach Schablone kleistert, Ist Nazi-Adolf hoch begeistert.

Und die Moral von der Geschicht', O Michel, glaub' dem Zauber nicht.

Die „Volks"-partei
Hier sieht man nun kurz vor dem Sterben Die Volkspartei um Adolf werben. Sie weiß nicht mehr wohin, wohin; Halb zog er sie, halb sank sie hin —

Wähl' Liste 1, hör' Du gut zu, Dann hast Du vor'm Faschismus Ruh.

Politisches Kabarett in Bildern

How she got wise, election pamphlet of the Social Democrat Workers Party, Netherlands, 1929.
1. Once upon a time there was a woman voting for the first time, but she was muddled and confused. 2. She asked her husband for advice, but he wouldn't help. 3. She asked a gentleman in a top hat, who answered that if she loved her Lord, she should vote for him. 4. She noticed the neighbours staring, and timidly asked them whether they knew who he was. 5. The neighbour answered that he was the clergyman, whose election platform was capital punishment and smallpox. 6. Then she saw a dazzling general who asked for her vote, but she answered that even she wasn't that stupid. 7. Next the poor woman met a pale gentleman in mourning, who told her to vote Calvinist. 8. But at a closer look, she realised he was her landlord! 'No, usurer, go and cheat somebody else!' 9. Then a curate told her to feel privileged to be able to vote for the Baron. 10. 'Baron!' the woman said, 'even I know he visited Mussolini in Rome!' 11. A gent overheard this, and said, 'thou hast escaped the threat of Rome!' 12. She replied that she wasn't interested in church learning, only in fair wages. 13. The gent slunk away, moaning, 'Woe! Protestant nation!' 14. Finally she bumped into a terrifying apparition, raving about murder and betrayal; recovering from her fright, she decided he must be a raving looney. 15. In the evening, she confessed shyly to her man, 'You can laugh at me all you want, but I now understand everything. I've decided to join the Party, and this summer I'll vote red!'

Political cabaret in pictures, Social Democrat election pamphlet, Germany, c. 1930.
1. (Hitler goes a-courting) NAZI FOREIGN POLICY. Here you see Adolf secretly spooning with our 'enemy', the French. At home, in the Prussian elections, however, he poses as a strict nationalist. 2. (Man handing over cheque: 'As long as there is no socialism') NAZI-SOCIALISM. The good Adolf promises anything and everything to the unemployed poor. Industry finances his election posters with a leer. 3. (Adolf as policeman: 'I have dressed myself well') THE NAZIS SETTLE IN. Adolf doesn't feel good in a policeman's uniform. Only when he gets to Braunschweig, as a member of the government, does he feel German, and a representative candidate. 4. (Coffin factory of the Third Reich. Here people are shot on the assembly line. 'Whoever ignores me gets shot') NAZI PROGRAMME. In the Third Reich we can look forward to the growth of the coffin industry. Because Best in Boxheim has decided, whoever is disobedient gets shot! 5. (The siege of Berlin) NAZI LEGALITY. Legality! Faithful to the constitution. So they swear solemnly every day. But what does an oath mean to these people, who quite 'legally' besiege Berlin? 6. NATIONAL CAPITAL. The gentleman who ruins himself is bailed out, like industry, by the government. The republic digs into its reserves — and goes bankrupt for its pains. 7. (The Communist. The party model) THE MODEL. Who is that scribbling? That idiot is a Communist. The more he follows the party model, the more Adolph gets his chance. 8. (Adolph, come and join us') THE 'PEOPLE'S PARTY'. Here you see the people's party shortly before its death. It is stumbling after Hitler. It doesn't know which way to turn — half is dragged along by Hitler, the other half collapses. And the moral of this story? Oh, Michael, don't believe in the magician! Listen everybody. Vote for List 1, and you won't be plagued by Fascism.

Facing page: Down with false slogans and knuckledusters, anti-Fascist pamphlet, Germany, 1930.
The truth is easily ignored
In a mouthful of empty words.
He who isn't able to persuade with facts
Will try to persuade by brutal acts.

1. Beware, the demagogue is in the land! Cunning, brazen, glib of tongue, he spreads slander, infamy and wrong. Arguments? His argument is fist and brawn! 2. The stormtrooper attacks, the chair is shattered and lame; the meeting hall is burnt to the ground. If they had their way, all Germany would look the same. 3. All hatred is aimed at the republic — he rails against it incensed. He desires a country of slaves, dominated by the spirit of obedience. 4. Disguising himself cunningly, he canvasses favour with one and all. He shakes hands with the worker, while the swindler has a ball. 5. He thinks: this kind of socialism I will profit by! An astute man supports the side on which his interests lie. 6. Thus Hugenberg took little Hitler to his bosom. He has paid dearly for this free blood transfusion. 7. Now Hugenberg is Hitler's puppet, lackey-like. I see him as the porter of the Third Reich. 8. Prince 'Auwi' approaches graciously, and the traitor falls upon one knee. 'Oh, join us please, the Third Reich just like an empire will be!' 9. A bumptious madman rules, the masses obediently yield. In spouting nonsense Hitler has cornered the field. 10. The Nazi sees a devil in the mirror with alarm. The only difference between reality and mirror image, though, is the uniform. 11. Despite all their hostile yelling, they are of the same blood. They are brothers-in-arms, kicking the republic into the mud. 12. People, fight back! Your rights are at stake. Kick them out, defend freedom for the republic's sake.

Fort mit Wort Schlag und Ring

Wer stets das Maul voll Phrasen nimmt,
Der sagt gewöhnlich, was nicht stimmt.

Wer nicht mit Gründen überzeugt
Der will daß man der Faust sich beugt.

Gebt Acht, der Hetzer ist im Land!
Gerissen, schnoddrig, wortgewandt,
Er Phrasen und Verleumdung prägt.
Beweise? – Sein Beweis, der „schlägt"

Der Sturmtrupp pfeift, das Stuhlbein kracht,
Entbrannt ist die Versammlungsschlacht.
War diese Horde Herr im Haus,
Ganz Deutschland sah wie das hier aus!

Der Republik gilt all sein Haß.
Auf sie schimpft er ohn Unterlaß.
Er will den Knechtsstaat, dessen Geist
Maulhalten und gehorchen' heißt.

Mit pfiffiger Verstellungskunst
Buhlt er um aller Stände Gunst.
Dem Arbeitsmann die Hand er drückt. –
Wie ist der Schieber da entzückt!

„Solch Sozialismus', denkt sich der,
ist wahrlich nicht von ungefähr'.
Der schlaue Mann gern unterstützt,
Was ihm ganz offensichtlich nützt.

Auch Hugenberg nahm einst mit Lust
Den Hitlerknaben an die Brust.
Für seines Blutes Transfusion
Erhält er jetzt gerechten Lohn.

Einst war der Nazi klein, er groß.
Jetzt ist er Hitlers Anhang bloß.
Im Geiste Hugenberg ich seh
Im „dritten Reiche' als Portier.

Naht huldvoll sich der Prinz Auwi,
Stracks fällt der Hetzer auf die Knie:
„Laß dich herab! Das dritte Reich,
Es wird dem Kaisertum ganz gleich!'

Ein aufgeblähter Narr regiert,
Die stumme Masse Volk pariert.
Im Unsinn reden – darauf Gift –
Hitler sein Vorbild übertrifft.

Hier sieht der Nazi teufelswild
Sein ganz getreues Spiegelbild.
Sein Ich, das er im Glas entdeckt
In anderer Uniform nur steckt.

Trotz allem feindlichen Gekreisch:
Die zwei sind Fleisch von einem Fleisch.
Stets ist das Bruderpaar vereint,
Gilt es der Republik als Feind.

Wehr ihnen, Volk! Schlag aus dem Feld
Den Prügelheld, den Phrasenheld!
Schirme dein Recht und gib den Sieg
Der Freiheit und der Republik!

AN IMAGE FOR CONTEMPLATION OF ARYAN ORIGIN

(According to the fascist race theory of what a true Aryan should look like)

БЕЛОКУР

BLOND LIKE HITLER

КАК ГИТЛЕР.

After the Signing of the Anglo–Soviet Agreement.

The Nazi press tricksters yell
THE ANGLO-SOVIET AGREEMENT MEANS NOTHING TO US.

СТРОЕН

WELL-SHAPED LIKE GOERING

КАК ГЕРИНГ.

Before the Signing of the Anglo–Soviet Agreement.

The Nazi press tricksters yelled
THE ANGLO-SOVIET NEGOTIATIONS regarding joint action can lead to no results.

КРАСИВ

HANDSOME LIKE GOEBBELS

КАК ГЕББЕЛЬС.

Here is what the Anglo-Soviet Agreement will mean.

Russian Second World War propaganda. From a collection of cartoons donated by Stalin to Lord Beaverbrook.
Facing page: artist of the above cartoon working with stencil.

L'ESPECULADOR

Avui us oferirà preus molt elevats pels vostres productes, perquè hi ha poc de tot i sap que podrà revendre'ls als consumidors a uns preus molt més alts encara....

però...

Demà quan vingui la normalitat i retorni l'abundància, us obligarà altra vegada, com feia abans, a vendre els productes a qualsevol preu i es cobrarà amb escreix el diner que ara us paga de més.

The Speculator, published by the Catalan government during the Civil War, Spain, *c.* 1936.

To all He will offer you high prices for your products, because there is a shortage of everything, and because he knows he can get even higher prices from the consumers...*but*...*Tomorrow* when everything is back to normal and there is plenty of everything available again, he will force you to lower your prices, as he did before, to get back the money he paid you over the odds.

1 A Canuto orden le han dado que vigile con cuidado.

2 Esa orden no la cumplió, pues dormido se quedó.

3 Silencioso y con sigilo se aproximó el enemigo.

INDISCIPLINA

Las órdenes son por algo I

4 Mientras Canuto roncaba un tanque se le acercaba.

5 Fué el ataque rechazado, mas Canuto así ha quedado.

A dire warning against falling asleep on guard, Republican strip, Spain, *c.* 1937.

Ton van Tast's front and back cover for a comic strip about the war, Netherlands, 1945 © Kompas.

1. 1945. Freedom for our country. Hip hip hooray! They've left our country...we're free again. (War picture book — keep it!)

2. Victory (top)...(right at bottom: the ruins) And we're handed herrings and bread, just as in Leiden in 1574...and everything else we've been hungering for....

ZEG, WEET JE 'T AL?

Want weet U 't al? Ja, weet U 't al?
Een inval is geen Carnaval
en geloof maar, binnen vier, vijf dagen
wordt 't Duitsche leger niet verslagen.

En weet U 't al? Ja, weet U 't al?
De Atlantik-wal, die staat pal!
Wie Duitschland uit ons land wil keeren,
moet 't tevens door de lucht probeeren.

Dus merkt U 't al? Ja, merkt U 't al?
Een vlieger is geen nachtegaal!
Die laat beslist iets anders vallen,
men merkt het niet alleen aan 't knallen.

Als zoo een vogel eens iets doet,
veeg je 't niet zoo maar van je hoed.
Zelfs d'allerdikste steenen muren
kunnen zoo'n vrachtje niet verduren.

Hoe zou het dàn wel moeten gaan
met huizen, die op palen staan,
waar kelders geen bescherming geven
en die reeds van den luchtdruk beven?

Stel U eens voor, zoo'n bomaanval
verbreekt IJmuiden's sluizenwal!
Dan bruist de Noordzee, losgelaten,
razend door d'Amsterdamsche straten!

De afsluitdijk gaat naar de maan,
er is geen houden of remmen aan!
Het land, ontwoekerd aan de zee,
wordt 'n massagraf voor mensch en vee!

Nu weet U 't wel, nu weet U 't wel!
Bij 'n inval komt U in de knel;
in plaats van 'n toppunt van verrukking
raakt Neêrland slechts in de verdrukking.

'Say, have you heard?', from *De Gil*, a Fascist comic, Netherlands, *c.* 1943.
1. Say, have you heard? 2. Say, have you heard? An invasion is no carnival, and don't you believe the German army can be beaten in four or five days. 3. Say, have you heard this one? The Atlantic wall stands firm, and anyone who wants to oust the Germans from our country will have to try it through the sky. 4. Say, have you noticed? An aviator is no nightingale, he drops something quite different, you can tell by the bangs. 5. When a bird like that drops something, you don't just wipe it off your hat. Even the thickest walls cannot resist such an attack. 6. Well, imagine what will happen to houses\built on piles, without cellars to give protection —houses which already shake under mere air pressure? 7. Just imagine a bomb attack that breaches the sea dykes of Ijmuiden — The North Sea will flood Amsterdam's streets! 8. The dam is gone, and the land, abandoned to the sea, becomes a mass grave for man and beast. 9. You'd better believe it, an invasion will oppress the Netherlands!

THE COMICS CODE

In 1954 the Cold War reached freezing point, and a wave of paranoia engulfed the USA. Hysterical tales appeared in the papers about a Red conspiracy, and everyone joined in the hunt for 'Communist infiltrators' who were out to weaken the country at the knees and corrupt America's youth, their object being to hand over the country to the Russians. Joseph McCarthy's Senate subcommittee headed the purge, and began a thorough investigation of the army and the news media. The hearings went on for months, and live TV and radio broadcasts engendered a hysterical atmosphere in which no one was innocent until proven not guilty. The media tried to clear themselves of blame by 'volunteering' to co-operate with the subcommittee in drawing up blacklists of journalists, film directors and others suspected of Communist sympathies. Hundreds of men and women, most of whose 'guilt' was never established, got the sack. Many of them never made it back.

Even the world of comics did not escape the witch hunt. The publication of F. Wertham's 'The Seduction of the Innocent' was more fat on the purge-fire. Wertham not only maintained that comics encouraged delinquency, but insisted on sinister aspects no one had ever dreamed of. Batman and his little friend Robin? Why, they were homosexuals, of course. Wonder Woman was not only a Lesbian but a sadist; and even Porky Pig, that most ingenuous of cartoon characters, was seen as an open invitation to buggery. Wertham's book was full of such accusations — primarily based on comics that had been out of circulation for eight years or

more. Despite the storm of protest the book drew from prominent psychologists, its effect was disastrous. The message was loud and clear: if you don't want your child to masturbate, poke out other children's eyes, become gay or be drawn towards sadism or masochism — then make sure it doesn't lay its sticky little hands on any comic books. Societies and women's institutes organized lectures and discussions which strengthened the best-selling book's message, and soon there was a virtual witch hunt, directed at comics and their creators. The 'ladies' movement' rallied to the cause. They pressured newspaper vendors and bookshops into banning comics. To make matters worse, the commission which had several years previously failed to discredit comics which were hauled out of the closet, given a good dusting, and, under the chairmanship of Senator Kefauver, given a new life as the Senate Subcommittee to Investigate Juvenile Delinquency. Of all the comic publishers, Bill Gaines of Educational Comics (EC) was to suffer most during the gruelling three-day hearing, which was broadcast live on TV. There was no hard evidence, but the prosecution called an impressive number of 'witnesses' and brandished reams of illustrative material torn out of context.

Although the subcommittee did not come to any verdict and the investigation did not lead to any prosecutions, the effect of the public hearings was enough to persuade many big publishers and distributors that they had better steer clear of certain comics. The comics industry, in a desperate attempt to stem the criticism, drew up its own blacklist and imposed a form of self-

18

censorship with a 'Comics Code Authority'. EC had to fold its most successful series and main bread-winners, 'Crypt of Terror' and 'Vault of Horror', because the use of the words 'terror' and 'horror' was prohibited for titles under the new code. The National Cartoonist Society, a group of prominent artists, protested loudly against the code and accused it of destroying the freedom of the press and freedom of expression. But they went unheard in the prevailing atmosphere of chauvinistic hysteria. The comics industry had to give in, and soon the Comics Code symbol adorned the covers of most comic books.

To give some idea of the nature of the self-censorship imposed by the Code, here are some of its more salient clauses:

■ Crimes shall never be presented in such a way as to create sympathy for the criminal, to promote distrust of the forces of law and justice, or to inspire others with a desire to imitate criminals.

■ Policemen, judges, government officials and respected institutions shall never be presented in such a way as to create disrespect for established authority.

■ In every instance good shall triumph over evil and the criminal be punished for his misdeeds.

■ No comic magazine shall use the word horror or terror in its title.

■ Nudity in any form is prohibited, as is indecent or undue exposure.

■ Females shall be drawn realistically without exaggeration of any physical qualities.

■ Illicit sex relations are neither to be hinted at nor portrayed. Violent love scenes as well as sexual abnormalities are unacceptable.

■ Passion or romantic interest shall never be treated in such a way as to stimulate the lower and baser emotions.

■ The treatment of love-romance stories shall emphasize the value of the home and the sanctity of marriage.

Most large publishers adhered to the rules, with the exception of two: the Dell Company, which published mainly romantic slush and children's cartoons about ducks and little pigs, and the Gilberton Company, which specialized in 'classics' — comics based on famous works of literature. Their magazines did not carry the Comics Code symbol — yet they did not suffer any perceptible drop in sales.

EC, however, was forced to change its style. A new series was launched in 1954 to fit the limitations of the Code, but it didn't take off and folded after barely one year. But then EC stumbled upon a new formula that was to give a new lease of life to the whole industry: 'Mad', which at the end of 1955, after twenty-three issues, was turned into an exclusively satirical magazine. Sales figures showed that 'Mad' had answered a new need. In an atmosphere of growing student involvement in ban-the-bomb and civil rights movements, 'Mad' hit some of the right notes in the escalating protest climate.

COMICS GO UNDERGROUND

'Mad's' editor, Harvey Kurzman, invented a totally new formula. The magazine simply ignored the Comics Code and turned to an adult audience. Everyday events and phenomena were satirized and made absurd: TV programmes, bestsellers, newspaper comic strips, movies, and even characters like Joe McCarthy. Its format and layout, too, were new. The traditional comic-magazine look was chucked out, and inside, the usual 'balloons' were replaced by more expansive texts underneath the pictures.

By 1956 EC had given up all its other publications to concentrate exclusively on 'Mad'. Then Kurzman fell out with his publisher, Bill Gaines. To safeguard his editorial freedom, Kurzman had demanded a larger stake for himself in the company, but Gaines refused, afraid that he would then lose control. Kurzman quit, and Gaines retained the rights to everything that had already appeared in 'Mad'. Having signed a contract with Ballantine Books, Gaines reprinted a lot of this material in paperback form. 'The Brothers Mad', 'The Mad Reader', 'Mad Strikes Back', 'Inside Mad' and 'Utterly Mad' were the first titles of a whole series, and have already passed their twenty-fifth editions. Kurzman never saw a penny of it. He was replaced as editor by Feldstein, another old EC hand.

In 1957 Kurzman launched a new magazine with backing from 'Playboy's' Hugh Hefner: 'Trump'. Three other ex-'Mad'men helped him to edit it: Jack Davis, Wally Wood and Bill Elder. Unfortunately, the magazine folded after two issues, because Hefner's own financial situation led him to withdraw his support. 'Trump's' staff, their ranks swollen by two new artists, Al Jaffee and Arnold Roth, decided to go it alone. Half a year after 'Trump' was played out they came up with another new magazine — 'Humbug', which showed itself to be more critical of society and the establishment. Unhampered by pressures and censorship from above, 'Humbug's' artists and editors could push their satirical humour to its limits, and the lampooning became more and more extreme. But independence had its drawbacks too: no publisher meant no efficient distribution. The magazine did not survive beyond the eleventh issue.

In 1958 — four years, that is, after the enforced retirement of the horror and terror magazines — publisher Jack Warren released the magazine 'Famous Monsters in Filmland', coinciding with the re-release of horror films of the thirties and forties on TV. As Warren used stills from old movies rather than cartoons, he could safely flaunt the Comics Code's laws — the Code did not apply to a magazine that contained no comics. This clever strategy helped to defeat the taboo against horror comics; the industry could breathe more freely and the public got what it wanted. 'Famous Monsters'' success and a new wave of horror movies produced in Hollywood in 1959 and 1960 — proof that there was a definite market for horror — eventually encouraged Jack Warren to defy the Comics Code openly a few years later by publishing new horror comics.

Now the time was ripe for something completely different. In 1960 Warren offered Kurzman the editorship of a new magazine: 'Help', subtitled 'for tired minds'. 'Help' bore Warren's unmistakable stamp in that it used old film stills with words added in balloons, just as 'Famous Monsters' had. Kurzman developed this method further by introducing photo strips (already popular in Italy as 'fumetti'), persuading well-known film stars to model for him.

'Help' was different: not only did it introduce a new style of drawings, it used offbeat adaptations of literary pieces — by H.G. Wells and Dickens for example — and brought back many long-forgotten artists. But 'Help's' biggest contribution was perhaps that it gave a whole new generation of artists a chance to get known. Skip Williams, Jay Lynch, Robert Crumb, Joel Beck and Gilbert Shelton laid down a new style for what was to become the 'underground' comic strip. With this new development of the political cartoon strip, 'Help' and its new crop of artists was way out ahead. 'Help's' readers, like 'Mad' readers, were mainly students, artists and intellectuals with 'tired minds', who responded avidly to the irreverent lampooning of institutions which they saw as absurd and alien.

Warren, who had become increasingly irritated with the irregularity of 'Help's' appearance, decided to fold it when publication had dwindled to one issue every three months. Kurzman and Bill Elder moved to 'Playboy' and created 'Little Annie Fannie', a sexy

An example of how Marvel Comics gave their strips a patriotic touch. *Superheroes win the war,* Marvel Comics, USA, 1942. © Marvel Comics.

satirical strip. Barbarella, drawn by Jean Claude Forest, first made her appearance in France in 1962 and then went off to the States with the 'Evergreen Review' a few years later. A vaguely feminist, definitely sex-pot archetype became a regular comic-strip fixture from then on, in America as well as Europe.

Wally Wood, Jack Davis and the others stayed with Warren and in the same year produced the first issue of 'Creepy' — a quarterly horror comic. The protests it raised weren't loud enough to do any harm, and Warren's distribution network was efficient enough to support it as well as a sister horror mag, 'Eerie'. These were a slap in the face for the already eroded authority of the Comics Code and prepared the way for the underground strip revolution, which was to stifle its dying whimpers once and for all.

Meanwhile, the youth movement — especially as found in the universities — had grown into a force to be reckoned with. It manifested itself in the 1960 demonstrations in San Francisco against the House Un-American Activities Committee and later in the Berkeley Free Speech Movement. Civil rights activists became more determined in the face of the openly racist and corrupt practices of Southern authorities as well as some sobering confrontations with police truncheons. Indeed, confrontation became the rallying cry of the young as they began to realize that there was no other way to tackle political and social abuses. All this activity heralded the coming of the new underground. The first tremors of the cultural revolution were felt in the student press.

Practically every college had its own paper, usually subsidized by the college and censored by the Dean. But gradually the mood of 'Mad', 'Trump' and 'Help' started infiltrating the student press. A case in point the 'Texas Ranger', the paper of the University of Texas at Austin, which grew more and more radical from 1958 to 1962, when Frank Stack and his successor Gilbert Shelton edited it. But the paper disappeared off the campus when it lost the battle against censorship, and its subsidy. The paper's staff stayed together, however, and set up the 'Austin Iconoclastic Magazine' which they financed, produced and distributed by themselves. It was a hit: sales were said to pass 10,000. Yet it too did not survive long — it slowly disintegrated through inefficient business management, and the staff went their different ways. Not however without leaving a very definite mark.

In 1961 Bill Killeen independently brought out 'The Charlatan' in Gainsville, Florida. Although no student himself, Killeen was well up on the student scene because of his connections with the 'Texas Ranger'. The students pounced eagerly on 'The Charlatan'. Killeen had managed to attract a good variety of artists, including some of his old colleagues on the 'Ranger', and 'Help' contributors like Jay Lynch, Art Spiegelman and Skip Williamson, and he also reprinted comics by Joel Beck from 'The Pelican' (the Berkeley student paper). Many bookshops refused to sell it and it was banned on most campuses. Nevertheless, the enterprising energy of the staff ensured a circulation of 5,000. Even more than its predecessor the 'Ranger', 'The Charlatan' was a foretaste of the comic revolution which got under way in underground publications

22 Bill Stout's anti-war comic strip, The Peacenuts, USA, 1967. © Handicap Publications.

produced by young people on their own terms.

The first true underground cartoon in comic-book form was published by Gilbert Shelton in 1962. It was called 'The Adventures of Jesus' and was drawn by Frank Stack — who called himself Foolbert Sturgeon for the occasion. It was cheaply produced, and only a few hundred xeroxed copies were circulated. In 1964 he tried again, this time with 'Godnose' by Jaxon, another veteran from the 'Texas Ranger'. This was an impeccably offset-printed affair, but did not run to more than 1,000 copies. Both cartoons were parodies of the Christian ethic. Godnose's motto was 'The nose is the anus of the soul'. Over ten years later, it was still being reprinted by the Rip Off Press.

The new approach was consolidated by 1965, when the underground press gave its first signs of life. This was the year Malcolm X was shot down, the year of the first bombings in Vietnam, and the year the New Left was born. The new Free Press became the mouthpiece for protest against the 'American Nightmare'. Offset printing made it easier and cheaper to produce one's own paper. More and more people seemed to feel the need to criticize the establishment and to discuss the possibility of a utopian society without Competition, Careers and Cancer. The mutterings became a movement: the underground press expressed the preoccupations of the movement…dropping out, happenings, urban warfare, pacifism, Black Power, anarchism, Zen, ecology, gay lib, women's lib — and comics! The new generation did not want to be swallowed up by the established order of things, and created its own lifestyle.

Most of the new papers, forerunners of the Underground Press Syndicate, came from the West Coast: the 'San Francisco Oracle', 'Open City', the 'Berkeley Barb' and the 'Los Angeles Free Press'.

The East Coast's contribution, at the end of 1965, was New York's 'East Village Other'. Its publisher, Walter Boward, was the first to come up with the suggestion for a federation of underground papers, to facilitate the exchange of material between them. The first national congress of the Free Press, in 1966, was attended by representatives of not more than ten papers, but their numbers increased rapidly, and soon the newly founded Underground Press Syndicate had 350 members, with a total circulation of an estimated five million throughout the United States and Europe. The aims of the movement reflect the mood and ideas of the time.

Here are some of the Syndicate's aims:
- To warn the 'Civilized World' of its impending collapse.
- To set up communications among aware communities outside the establishment.
- To note and chronicle events leading to the collapse.
- To observe facts which reflect, and unveil in advance, the undercurrents dangerous to freedom.
- To advise intelligently to prevent rapid collapse and make transition possible.
- To seek out others of like thoughts and to recognize each tribe.
- To prepare ways of living should the machine stop.
- To advise how to reinstate balance to the ecology.

CHARLATAN
☆☆ AMERICA'S NO. 1 COLLEGE MAGAZINE
50¢

The Religious Issue

FEATURING
God Nose

Jaxon's design for cover of *Charlatan*, an American college magazine, USA, 1962.

EVERGREEN
EVERGREEN REVIEW NO. 37 SEPTEMBER 1965 ONE DOLLAR

MAIS, LA, CLE?

NE SUIS-JE PAS LE SERRURIER DU PALAIS? J'AI LE DOUBLE DE TOUTES LES CLES … MÊME DE LA PLUS SECRÈTE …

BARBARELLA IS HERE!
Barbarella, on her way to international fame, in *Evergreen*, USA, 1965 (originally published in France in 1964).
'But the key?' 'Am I not the locksmith of the palace? I have a duplicate of every key, even the most secret one…'

UNITED CARTOON WORKERS OF AMERICA

In the years that followed, the political consciousness of the movement grew into outright revolt: more and more sectors of the establishment came under attack.

The underground press was instantly recognizable, not only in its design — its wild use of colour and eye-catching visual effects which exploited the possibilities of photo-offset printing to the full — but also, of course, by its radical editorial content.

In 1966 the Parallax publishing company introduced a new kind of political satirical strip. Produced by D.J. Arneson and Tony Tallarico, they starred famous politicians, like Lyndon B. Johnson and Teddy Kennedy, in superhero attire. The series, called The Great Society, caught a lot of attention, but funds soon ran out and it folded after a few issues.

The 'East Village Other' was one of the first underground papers to publish comic strips. The first of these was 'The Adventures of Captain High' by Bill Beckman. A psychedelic take-off of Marvel's superheroes, its lack of artistic quality was more than compensated for by its theme — the taboo subject of marijuana.

Many of the artists who created strips for the 'EVO', like Alan Schmer and Kim Deitch, were painters who really belonged to the Pop Art school. Deitch, inspired by the Captain High strip, turned out the first real underground serial comic strip, 'Sunshine Girl'. Like Bill Beckman's work, 'Sunshine Girl' was drawn in an abstract, psychedelic style.

By 1967, more and more talented artists appeared on the scene, all with a heightened political awareness. Well-known names from this period include Trina Robbins, whose comic-strip heroine, Suzie Slumgoddess, started life as an advertisement for her boutique; and Manuel Rodriguez, ex-member of the Road Vultures, a Buffalo motorbike gang. He went to New York to work for the 'EVO', and his first comic, 'Zodiac Mindwarp', was published in 1967. The public wasn't ready for it, and just about the entire print run ended up on the dust heap. The next year, in February, all copies of the current issue of the 'EVO' were confiscated because of a sexy frame in one of the strips by Spain, as Rodriguez now called himself. The next issue carried the offending picture on its cover, in the form of a series of numbers, with the caption 'You can be arrested for linking up these numbers'. Readers were urged to send the completed drawings to the Public Prosecutor. The court case ended in acquittal for publisher and artists.

Spain's comics were from the start distinguished by their strong political involvement. His work not only appeared in the underground press, but also embellished all kinds of pamphlets and manifestos issued by radical action groups.

Robert Crumb was to be another important contributor to the 'EVO', which had already published one

of his comic strips taken over from Yarrowstalks. When he too turned up in New York, he joined the talented groups at 'EVO' and designed dazzling covers, illustrations and strips.

In 1968 Vaughn Bode came to New York and talked 'EVO's' business manager into producing a whole magazine devoted exclusively to comic strips. And so the 'Gothic Blimp Works' appeared on the scene with a three-colour cover and artwork. Just about every 'new' comic-strip artist living in New York at the time contributed: Roger Brand, Spain, Trina, Kim and Simon Deitch, Gilbert Shelton, Willy Murphy, John Tompson, Art Spiegelman, Justin Green, Bill Griffith, Vaughn Bode and Robert Crumb. Even West Coast artists joined in by mail: S. Clay Wilson, Robert Williams, George Metzger and Rory Hayes. After three issues, Kim Deitch took over as editor from Vaughn Bode. At the end of 1969 seven issues had appeared, and the paper's success was so great that an eighth issue was compiled from material previously published in the 'EVO'.

Although the underground press had agreed to the unrestricted exchange of material among the papers, most articles and editorials proved to be of limited local interest. The comic strips on the other hand did enjoy a nationwide audience, and their creators soon gained recognition throughout the country. One of the most widely syndicated strips, not surprising in view of

its subject, was Spain's personal interpretation of the Comics Code censorship.

On the West Coast, a thriving new industry sprang up around the psychedelic flower-power centre of Haight Ashbury. A number of artists, who had made a name for themselves by working on the 'Texas Ranger' and other papers, found themselves involved in designing posters for Chet Helms's rock concerts at San Francisco's Family Dog. The production of the posters was supervised by Jaxon, and they turned out to be so sought-after that they soon made their way into the shops. Just as the protest songs of the mid-sixties were giving way to the acid rock of the Grateful Dead, Jefferson Airplane and Quicksilver Messenger Service, so the graphics of the new posters reflected the psyche-delic mood of the time. Dozens of small printers mushroomed up out of nowhere to cater to the ensuing poster craze that made its way over to Europe in no time. Posters by young designers like Victor Moscoso, Greg Irons, Steve Wilson and Rick Griffin gained worldwide recognition.

Don Schenker's Print Mint played an important part in the rise of the comic underground, first solely as distributor, and then, after a small press had been rigged up, as printer as well. In 1966 Schenker had already published a couple of comics by Joel Beck — 'Lenny of Laredo', which was inspired by the life of the master of black humour, Lenny Bruce, and

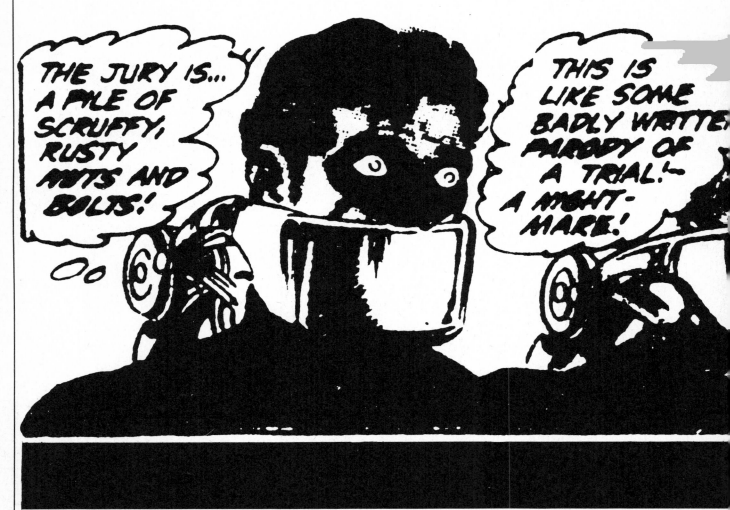

'Marchin' Marvin'. Towards the end of 1967 the Print Mint produced Robert Crumb's first comic book, 'Zap no. 1'. (It was in fact the second issue, but the originals of the first book planned by Crumb had mysteriously gone missing. Crumb later found some photocopies of these, which he published as 'Zap no. 0'.)

Moscoso and Griffin had also toyed for a time with the idea of a comic book of their own, but after seeing Zap they decided to join forces with Crumb. Besides a new comic magazine, the 'Yellow Dog', the Print Mint also distributed the remaining stock of Gilbert Shelton's 'Feds and Heads', which had been independently published by Shelton himself and which he had tried to flog during the 1968 Democratic Convention demonstrations in Chicago. Another artist hawking his wares among the demonstrating Weathermen and Yippies was Jay Lynch, who together with Skip Williamson had collected the first issue of 'Bijou Comics' from the printer.

Then a number of artists fell out with Schenker over the high cut of the profits claimed by Print Mint, and Gilbert Shelton and Jaxon got together to set up their own publishing company, the Rip Off Press. This was planned as a kind of artists' co-operative on a profit-sharing basis. The Rip Off Press was a welcome alternative to exploitation; less commercial artists, often attached to political organizations, were also drawn to Rip Off in great numbers. One of the press's

first ventures was a special comic-strip supplement for the SDS magazine 'Radical America'.

The creation of the Rip Off Press underlines a change within the underground movement which had been brewing for some time, but which first led to an actual split around 1968 or 1969. Part of the underground began to face the political consequences of something that had begun as a spontaneous cultural revolution. An increasing number of underground papers fell under the influence of opposing ideologies, and the polarization within the movement drove the different groups farther and farther apart. On one side, the isolationism of the movement was expressed by advocates of alternative lifestyles who sought escape in communal dropping-out and meditation; on the other side there were those political radicals who glorified the socialist third-world liberation movements and urban guerillas. An artist who made the subject of colonialism and anti-imperialism his own was Rius; based in Mexico, he publicized in his comic strips the history of Cuba, the Chicanos and the Tupamaros, and his strips were published by the New Left papers in America.

Even the commercial superheroes were given a face-lift. Subjects like the environment, women's liberation, Black Power and Vietnam were no longer taboo. Marvel Comics — generally more at home in the fifth dimension — allowed Captain America to question his

own ideas about democracy and justice on earth. In 1970 readers were able to see Green Arrow and his mate Green Lantern standing in the dock, handcuffed and gagged, before a vicious judge and a jury of robots — clearly a satire on the notorious Chicago Eight trial, when eight political activists were accused of being responsible for the 1968 Chicago demonstrations. To raise money to cover the Eight's defence costs, the 'Conspiracy' (Kathleen Cleaver and Susan Sontag) published a comic book consisting of work by well-known underground artists.

The political strip was manipulated with increasing professional skill, and more and more people started to use comics to express political ideas. Ron Turner, who was working at the Berkeley Ecology Center, brought out 'Slow Death Funnies' — a collection of comics by well-known cartoonists attacking the eco-logical mess created by the capitalist system. It was so successful that it fathered a whole new publishing business, Last Gasp — Eco Funnies. Small comics publishers sprang up all over the States: the Krupp Comic Works in Milwaukee; the L A Comic Book Company in Los Angeles; Armadillo Comics in Austin, Texas; and the San Francisco Comic Book Cy in San Francisco. The mostly Marxist-inspired women's movement also exerted a strong influence. The separatist ideas that grew out of Women's Lib inspired a number of comics by women: at first, these only made a hesitant appearance in the early Women's Lib papers, but soon they were producing complete comic books.

The 'underground strip', so new a few years before, was already passé, and few of the artists associated with its birth could still find grace with the radicalized editors of the underground press after 1970. Trina Robins went on to draw the adventures of Belinda Berkeley, a revolutionary lady. Others who were still published in the radical papers were Spain Rodriguez, Skip Williamson, Bill Crawford, Lundgren, Bobby London and Adams.

In order to protect themselves against piratical presses which reprinted material without bothering with copyright, a number of underground artists founded the 'United Cartoon Workers of America'. In a corner of their comic book covers the symbol of the Comics Code was replaced by the symbol of their union: a draughtsman's pen in a clenched fist.

The underground strip was regarded as a powerful and subversive tool, able to change political as well as cultural conceptions. Quality was therefore a means, not an end, which went to show that comics were not reserved for those who had been taught to draw them. And that alone makes the underground strip a vitalizing and liberating force.

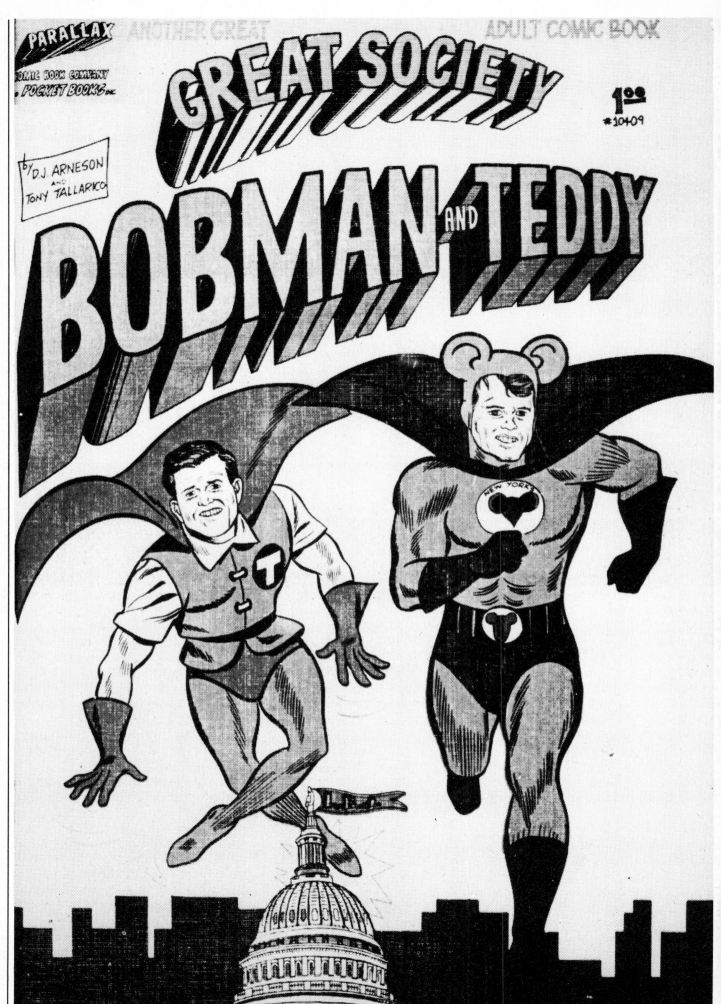

Cover of a *Great Society Comic Book* by D.J. Arneson and Tony Tallarico, USA, 1966. © Parallax Comic Books Inc.

HER NAME IS **BELINDA BERKELEY** AND SHE'S WORRIED BECAUSE AFTER 4 YEARS OF STRUGGLING THROUGH COLLEGE FOR A DEGREE SHE CAN'T GET A DECENT PAYING JOB ANYWAY, AND HER OLD MAN WANTS HER TO JUST TAKE **ANY OLD JOB** SO SHE CAN SUPPORT HIM WHILE HE WRITES THAT NOVEL, AND NOW THEY TELL HER THOSE BIRTH CONTROL PILLS SHE'S TAKING MAY GIVE HER **CANCER**, BUT SHE CAN'T STOP BECAUSE HER OLD MAN SAYS HE ISN'T READY FOR THE RESPONSIBILITY OF A FAMILY, AND THEY DON'T HAVE MALE CONTRACEPTIVE PILLS ON THE MARKET YET, AND SHE KIND OF WONDERS IF THEY EVER **WILL**, AND SHE THINKS...

I THINK I'M BEING **USED**...?

SO ONE DAY, WHEN SOMEONE HANDED HER A LEAFLET ON A STREET CORNER...

INTERNATIONAL WOMEN'S DAY! WOMEN'S LIBERATION! PERHAPS I'LL FIND THE ANSWER **THERE**!

AT THE RALLY...

BUY A PAPER? SPECIAL WOMEN'S LIBERATION ISSUE!

UH... OKAY...

HEY, THIS IS A **SOCIALIST** PAPER! IT'S NOT ABOUT WOMEN'S LIBERATION AT ALL! O WELL, MAYBE THE SPEAKERS...

AH YES, THE SPEAKERS...

OFF THE PIGS!!

POWER TO THE PEOPLE!

FREE LOS SIETE!

BUT WHAT ABOUT **WOMEN**?

WE MUST ALL WORK **TOGETHER** FOR THE REVOLUTION... STAND BEHIND OUR MEN IN THEIR STRUGGLE... AND THEN, **AFTER** THE REVOLUTION, WE CAN WORK ON BEING FREE!

SO SHE LEAVES, TIRED AND PUZZLED... NOBODY SAID MUCH ABOUT ABORTION OR WHY SHE CAN'T GET A DECENT WAGE, BUT A WHOLE LOT OF PEOPLE TRIED TO SELL HER ON CAUSES THAT WEREN'T REALLY HERS AND SHE THINKS...

I THINK I'M BEING **USED**...?

TRINA

IS BELINDA BERKELEY BEING USED? WHAT **ABOUT** ABORTION, ANYWAY? WILL HER OLD MAN GET AN HONEST JOB? FOLLOW HER ADVENTURES IN **IT AIN'T ME, BABE**!

Trina's Belinda Berkeley, USA, 1970. © It Ain't Me Babe.

Spain, cover of *Zodiac Mindwarp*, USA, 1967. © Manuel Rodriguez.

"THAT IS NOT DEATH WHICH CAN ETERNAL LIE; AND WITH STRANGE AEONS EVEN DEATH MAY DIE"

FROM THE NECRONOMICON BY THE MAD ARAB ABDUL ALHAZRAD

WE SIT ... IN PATIENCE

WAITING FOR THE DAY.....

WHEN WE SHALL REINHERIT THE EARTH

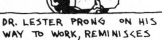

YES LESTER, THE YEARS HAVE BEEN KIND TO YOU,...YOU HAVE DONE YOUR WORK AND DONE IT WELL

DR. LESTER PRONG ON HIS WAY TO WORK, REMINISCES

REMEMBER BEFORE, THE WAY THINGS USED TO BE REMEMBER HOW DISGUSTING THE PHANTOM LADY WAS

AND OH! THOSE HORRID E.C.s WHAT A RELIEF IT WAS TO DRIVE TALES FROM THE CRYPT OFF THE STANDS

AND REMEMBER HOW INSIDIOUSLY YOUNG MINDS WERE EXPOSED TO CARNAL KNOWLEDGE DISGUISED AS BATMANS ARMPIT IN REALITY A BLATANT FEMALE VAGINA

BUT THE GOOD DR. WERTHAM PUT A STOP TO IT..... AND EVER SINCE WE'VE KEPT THINGS IN LINE, OBSCURING AN OVER SUCULENT TITTY ERASING AN OVER MOLDY CORPSE

THAT NOISE! WHAT IS IT?

CODE AUTHORITY

YOU THOUGHT YOU HAD RID YOURSELF OF US LESTER, BUT NOW WE'VE COME FOR YOU!

GULP! AUT!

SLISH SPLOP SKRGE

HEH HEH SCREE

YAAAAAAAGH

NO!...PLEASE I DIDN'T MEAN...

The Comics Code as seen by Spain, USA, 1968. © Manuel Rodriguez.

Cover of *Yellow Dog*, USA, 1968. © Print Mint.

The True Story of the **cuban revolution**

"Ariel"

THERE HE MEETS A YOUNG ARGENTINIAN DOCTOR NAMED ERNESTO GUEVARA, THEY BECOME CLOSE FRIENDS AND FIDEL NICKNAMES HIM "CHE"

CASTRO AND HIS FOLLOWERS MAKE PLANS TO INVADE CUBA. THEY DECIDE TO LAND IN ORIENTE, AND TAKE TO THE HILLS.

TWO YEARS LATER THEY ARE RELEASED FROM PRISON. IT WAS THE 15TH OF MAY, 1955

AFTER TRYING TO FIND A SOLUTION TO CUBA'S DILEMA, CASTRO DECIDES THAT THE ONLY SOLUTION IS THE ARMED STRUGGLE. HE VOLUNTARILY EXILES TO MEXICO AND STARTS CONSPIRING.

MILITARY TRAINING IS TAKEN WITH THE HELP OF "ALBERTO BAYO" SPANISH GENERAL EXILED IN MEXICO.

BEFORE LEAVING, CASTRO WRITES A LETTER TO BATISTA.

BATISTA, AFTER READING CASTRO'S LETTER DECIDES TO IGNORE HIS WARNING.

IN THE MEANTIME.... CUBANS CONTINUED TO DIE IN THE STREETS

AT LAST ON NOV. 24TH, 1956 THEY LEAVE MEXICO FROM THE PORT OF VERACRUZ. 82 PATRIOTS TAKE TO THE OPEN SEA IN THE MIDDLE OF THE NIGHT.

CONTINUED...

Second page of a comic strip about the Cuban Revolution, USA, 1971. © Hooka.

THIS IS A MAP OF URUGUAY. HALF THE POPULATION LIVES IN MONTEVIDEO BUT THE GUERRILLA WAS BORN IN THE WEST, IN ARTIGAS.

IN JUNE, 1962, THE PEASANTS OF THE SUGAR CANE MARCHED ON THE CAPITAL TO DEMAND AGRARIAN REFORMS. THEY ARE POOREST PEOPLE IN THE COUNTRY.

CANE WORKERS WORK ONLY 4 MONTHS A YEAR AND STARVE THE REST. THEY ASKED FOR LAND BUT NO ONE IN THE CAPITAL PAID ATTENTION TO THEM. ON THE CONTRARY, THEY ATTACKED THEM AND THE POLICE SHOT AT THEM.

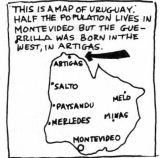

THE ONLY THING THEY GOT OUT OF THE MARCH WAS APPROVAL OF AN 8 HR. DAY AND THEY RETURNED HOME DISAPPOINTED. THERE WERE MORE THAN 2,000 FAMILIES AND THEY WERE LED BY RAUL SENDIC, A LAW STUDENT.

CAN YOU IMAGINE? WE HAVE PEASANTS IN URUGUAY

A YEAR GOES BY AND IN JULY 1963 A STRANGE NEWS ITEM APPEARS IN THE PAPERS: 12 RIFLES WERE STOLEN FROM THE RIFLE CLUB IN NEW HELVETIC. ONE OF THE ASSAILANTS WAS SENDIC...

SENDIC? HE MUST BE ONE OF FIDEL'S PEOPLE.

AND THAT'S WHERE THE STORY SEEMS TO END; THE POLICE LOSE TRACK OF HIM AND NOTHING HAPPENS DURING THE FOLLOWING MONTHS... UNTIL IN DECEMBER OF THE SAME YEAR SOMETHING UNHEARD OF OCCURS...

MERRY CHRISTMAS

TEN YOUTHS TAKE OVER A TRUCK FULL OF WINES, TURKEYS AND XMAS FOODS AND DISTRIBUTE THEM IN POOR NEIGHBORHOODS IN MONTEVIDEO. THEY DECIDE TO CALL THEMSELVES THE "TUPAMAROS."!

¿TUPA QUE?

THEY LOOK MORE LIKE SANTA CLAUS TO ME.

TUPAC-AMARO WAS AN INCA INDIAN CHIEFTAN WHO LED A REBELLION IN 1780 AGAINST THE SPANIARDS IN PERU; DEFEATED HE WAS DRAWN AND QUARTERED IN THE PUBLIC PLAZA.

LIKE HIM, THE TUPAMAROS ARE FIGHTING FOR INDEPENDENCE.

THIS ACTION, WORTHY OF A ROBIN HOOD, IS FOLLOWED BY MORE THEFTS OF GUNS, GRENADES, AND DYNAMITE ACROSS THE COUNTRY. THE POLICE CAN'T FIGURE ANYTHING OUT. UNDER PRESSURE FROM THE U.S.A. THE GOVERNMENT BREAKS RELATIONS WITH CUBA LOOKING FOR ANYONE BUT THEMSELVES TO BLAME.

BREAK WITH CUBA... BREAK WITH CUBA... BREAK....

THIS MEASURE IS GREETED WITH BOMBINGS OF YANKEE BUSINESSES, BURNING OF YANKEE DIPLOMAT'S CARS, BURNING OF CANE FIELDS, MASS MEETINGS AND MORE HOLD-UPS OF BANKS AND ARMORIES.

1965 AND **1966** SAW A QUICK SUCCESSION OF BANK ROBBERIES AND ARM THEFTS; ALSO THE EXPROPIATION OF POLICE UNIFORMS FOR FUTURE ACTIONS.

I DON'T THINK ITS FUNNY

ALL OF THESE ACTIVITIES ARE ATTRIBUTED TO THE TUPAMAROS BY THE POLICE, BECAUSE OF THEIR "PERFECT ORGANIZATION" GOOD EDUCATION AND THEIR "HUMAN TOUCH"

THEY HAD TO BE TUPAS; THEY CALLED ME BY MY NAME!

Two pages from a comic book about the Tupamaros, USA, 1971. © NACLA.

Skip Williamson's cover of *Conspiracy Capers*, USA, 1969. © The Conspiracy.

Cover of *My Love*, Marvel Comics, USA, 1971. © Marvel Comics Group.

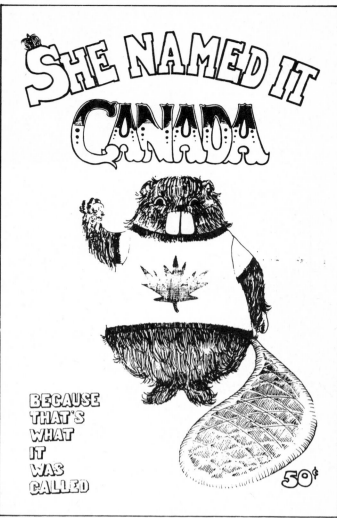

Alternative history books become a trend. Cover of a comic strip about Canada, Canada, 1971. © The Corrective Collective.

Cover of a comic book about Cuba by Rius, USA, 1970. © Leviathan.

The Marvel superheroes become radicalized, USA, 1970. © National Periodical Publications.

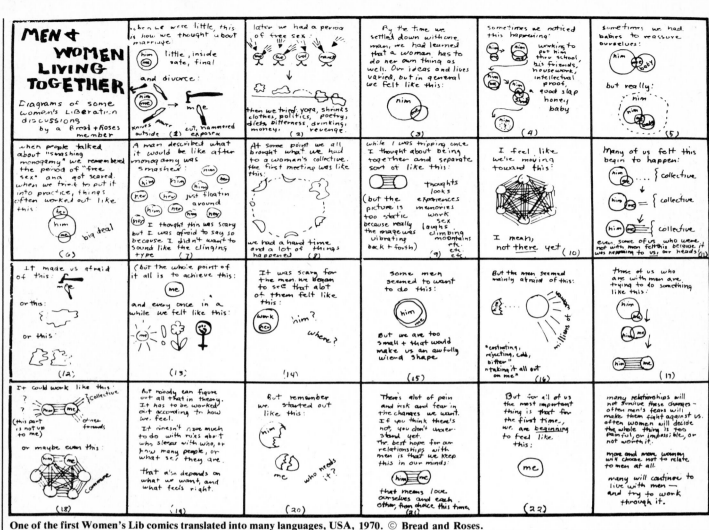

One of the first Women's Lib comics translated into many languages, USA, 1970. © Bread and Roses.

Women's Lib comic from *Everywoman*, USA, 1971.
© *Everywoman*.

Trina, the liberation of Suzie Slumgoddess, USA, 1970. © Trina.

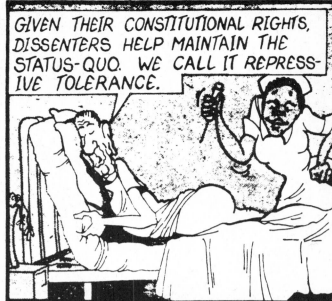

'A face lift' by Frank Adams, USA, 1969. © San Diego Free Press.
Facing page: Tricky Dick visits San Francisco, USA, 1968. © *San Francisco Express Times.*

TRICKY DICK VISITS S.F.

WE WILL NOT BE INTIMIDATED BY A LOT OF THUGS AND ANARCHISTS.

THE UNITED STATES.... IS THE LAND OF **GOLDEN** OPPORTUNITY!

PEOPLE ARE TRYING TO DESTROY THE SACRED PRINCIPLES AND TRADITION BY WHICH WE LIVE. (sic)

WHEN I AM ELECTED, I WILL FOLLOW THE GREAT TRADITION OF MY OFFICE AND DESTROY 'EM

Rufus, the radical reptile, created by Bill Crawford, USA, 1970. © *Berkeley Tribe.*

THE POLLUTION SOLUTION

Pollution solution, USA, 1970. © Yossarian.

The establishment hits back, USA, 1969.

42 Cover of *Left-Field Funnies*, USA, 1971. © Bobby London.

COMICS
CAN ATTACK THE
ESTABLISHMENT

Strips rarely attack individuals, but focus on characters representing whole groups or classes. By using the subversive power of humour, comics can attack the establishment, and express criticism of institutions which would remain unassailable by any other means. This type of humour is often the only opening for criticism in totalitarian states. In Spain under Franco, for example, 'Hermano Lobo' had a ludicrously high circulation for a humorous paper because of its covert criticism of the authorities. Another recent example is the Portuguese paper 'Comercio do Funchal'. Under the Fascist regime it was full of jolly funnies and jokes, but after 25 April 1974 it immediately transformed itself into a radical political paper. Ironically, it was also one of the first papers to be banned by the MFA (Armed Forces Movement).

The comic strip has always been a medium of the proletariat — the middle and upper classes have tended to treat it as a cast-off of the advertising world. It was equally rejected by the traditional movements of the Left after the war. In fact, it must be said that magazines like 'Mad' and 'Help' did more to influence the growth of youth rebellion than the dogmatic establishment Left. The new culture and lifestyle which grew out of the fifties and sixties inspired the birth of the 'New Left' — and not vice versa.

Political comic strips also played an important propagandist role during and after the Chinese cultural revolution. Hundreds of comics were issued and distributed among millions to spread 'correct' political ideas. Similarly, in Allende's Chile many strips were published with the aim of instilling a revolutionary consciousness in the people. Comic strips equally played an important role in Angola. The struggle between the Angolan liberation movements and the Portuguese colonial army escalated towards the end of the sixties, and the battle was fought not only with bullets: propaganda was used extensively by both sides. In the areas they had liberated the MPLA distributed an alphabet book which read like an anti-colonialist comic strip, and the Portuguese army retaliated with pamphlets in which simple strips exhorted the people not to collaborate with the guerillas.

Although we cannot show such examples from every country in the world, it is clear that the political comic strip is not a Western monopoly. For example, look at the serialized strip from the journal of the Moroccan Socialist opposition party.

Bourgeois behaviour towards strikers before and after the coup (PIDE stands for the hated secret police), Portugal, 1974. © *Combate.*

Situationist poster illegally distributed in and around the universities, Portugal, 1971.
Meanwhile in the Bacchanalian dance of truth...
1. 'It was a party without beginning or end; I saw no one and everyone, because every individual was lost in that fluctuating innumerable throng. I spoke to everybody without remembering what anyone or even what I myself said, as my attention was absorbed at every stage by new events, by unexpected news.' —Bakunin, *Confession.* 2. 'I saw him (Bakunin) for the first time in sixteen years. I have to confess he made a good impression on me, better than he did before (...) He is one of the few people I know who seemed to be progressing rather than regressing after sixteen years.' —Marx, letter to Engels, 4 November 1864.

Facing page: Vicente Barão's manikins in *Comercio do Funchal,* Portugal, 1974. © *Comercio do Funchal.*

GOD IN FRANCE
1. 'I've just been to see the parties of the extreme left.' 'Do they really eat little children?' 'Every child they catch sight of, and they also kill dogs, torture cats and play into the "reaction's" hands.' 2. 'Proclaim immediately a national minimum wage!' (King rejects this.) 3. 'Well, a small minimum wage as the kingdom's economy cannot carry a large increase.' (King repeats.) 4. 'Let's say *one* coin per citizen.' (King repeats.) 5. 'I smell extreme left-wing militants.' 'Yes.' 6. 'Speak up! What do you want, O voice of the darkness?' 7. 'Jesus! An aggressive ideology!'

Bonecos de Vicente Barão

no reino de frança

Clandestine stickers distributed before the coup, Portugal, 1973.
1. Emigration is no solution. 2. Stop being a slave. Stand up and fight! 3 & 4. The weapons we steal are for our liberation. The weapons of the people.

EMIGRAR NÃO É SOLUÇÃO

DEIXA DE SER ESCRAVO
ERGUE-TE
E LUTA!

AS ARMAS QUE ROUBARMOS SERVEM PARA A NOSSA LIBERTAÇÃO

AS ARMAS QUE ROUBARMOS SERVEM PARA A NOSSA LIBERTAÇÃO

O programa do MDP/CDE em imagens

II VIAS E OBJECTIVOS NA TRANSIÇÃO PARA UM ESTADO AMPLAMENTE DEMOCRÁTICO. 1. — Vias e objectivos políticos. — 1.4. — Liberdade religiosa. — Reconhecimento e garantia de completa liberdade religiosa para todos os portugueses, implicando o direito de professar ou não professar ou de contestar qualquer religião ou opinião religiosa, o direito de difundir doutrinas religiosas e o direito dos cidadãos se organizarem em comu-

nidades, associações ou outros institutos com fins religiosos. — Estabelecimento do regime jurídico da separação da Igreja do Estado. Neutralidade e laicidade do Estado perante quaisquer crenças, igrejas, religiões ou práticas religiosas. — Regulamentação civil do direito do divórcio, independentemente de quaisquer considerações ou limitações de natureza canónica. — Introdução de um espírito

novo nas relações diplomáticas com o Vaticano, através da revisão da Concordata, de forma que este instrumento jurídico passe a corresponder à nova situação política de democratização e descolonização em que o povo português está empenhado. Nomeadamente, abolição do acordo missionário, direito ao divórcio, eliminação do ensino da religião nas escolas públicas, não ingerência do Governo na nomeação de funcionários eclesiásticos.

Political programme of the centre party MDP/CDE, Portugal, 1975.
For religious freedom, yes, no to the *mafiosos*! Truth for the immigrants! For a Portuguese Socialism without the old barriers!

46

From the right-wing paper *Qué Pasa*. Spain, 1975.
'Rice with milk… rice with milk… I want to
marry a girl from Portugal—like this one—yes!
Like that one—No!'

The fall of Spinola, Portugal, 1975. © *Spartacus*.

100. Once in the village the aggressors are like a wild bull in a ring of fire. As Chairman Mao says: **"The flexible employment of his [a commander] forces is the most important means of changing the situation as between the enemy and ourselves and of gaining the initiative."** Kao Chuan-pao and some militiamen dive into the tunnel to take their positions, watching the enemy carefully.

101. When the enemy enter the village, Chuan-pao shouts through a bamboo communications tube: "Attention every fighting group! Ready for independent combat. Change position after each shot. Make every bullet count."

102. The enemy draw to within 50 metres, the militia watching silently. Then the order "Fire!" is relayed throughout the tunnel complex.

103. Bullets fly at the enemy from everywhere. Kang is ordered to go with his machine-gun to fire from a height, and climbs between two walls.

104. Kang again shifts into a tree hollow and fires down on the enemy.

Covers of comic books published after the Cultural Revolution, China, *c.* 1970-72.

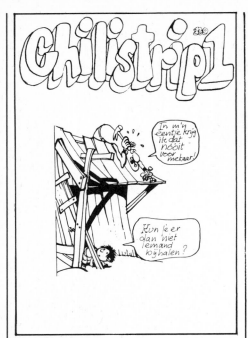

Cover of a Dutch translation of a Chilean comic book on the politics of property ownership, Chile, 1971.

Two pages from MPLA alphabet, Angola *c.* 1967.

Comic strip from the tolerated Moroccan opposition, Morocco, 1975.
1. 'You can come and look at the Minister of Information.' 2. Flush her please (TV). Please use morning and night (loo paper). Information by deformation. Signed: des Cartes. 3. This is the waiting room. (On the block: national press). 4. *Censored.

1. 'I say, I'm clean out of cash. I think I ought to try and find some work here.' 2. 'What kind of luggage have you got?' 'Two suitcases and a rucksack.' 3. 'No! I mean diplomas.' 'I haven't got any.' 4. 'Then it'll be easy for you to find work at the Ministry of Education. We'll go there tomorrow.'

Portuguese Army propaganda aimed at Angolans living in the Liberated Territories, Angola, *c.* 1970.
1. Terrorists only bring war and suffering. The head of the village and others must capture terrorists that try to invade the aldeamentos (protected villages). Those who help the terrorists will be punished. Those who capture terrorists will be rewarded and will live in peace. 2. Warning to the population: the people must go to the aldeamento. In the jungle is war, in the aldeamento is peace. 3. The army will escalate its pursuit of the enemy. Abandon the terrorists and go to the aldeamento. All people found outside the aldeamento will be treated like the enemy. The army is only in pursuit of people outside the aldeamento. Go to the aldeamento to be safe.
4. People living in the aldeamento enjoy the protection of the army and the government. Call up all the people to come to the aldeamento. There they will be able to live in peace and freedom. If anyone comes into the aldeamento whom you have never seen before, tell the authorities and the militia. Strangers only want to harm you. Help to protect your aldeamento.

PROVOKING THE SYSTEM

Everywhere we go, we are programmed by a relentless stream of coded images. Some of these have their uses, like signposts and traffic signs. But the advertising hoardings are another story. A mercenary army of media-men, industrialists and psychological quacks do nothing but dream up new ways of blitzing our senses into conformity. The advertising industry becomes more grotesque by the day, and every product reflects a 'need' implanted in our brains by the dream factories. These tricks and techniques combine with the pseudo-events reported by the newspapers and dished up on the telly to bring us 'reality': an endless graphic tear-off calendar of news which becomes a substitute for reality, your reality. It has no bearing on our everyday existence on the factory floor, in the kitchen. The dominant system, as it exists with subtle variations throughout the world, provokes resistance and protest everywhere.

The first rumbles of discontent at the growing automation of life were heard from the rebelling youth gangs of the late fifties. Teds and Mods were working-class youths who were bored out of their minds and tried to bring excitement into their lives with aggressive behaviour and flashy gear. Existentialism had already found a number of victims among the offspring of the middle classes, and the first beatniks hitchhiked their way through Europe. The ban-the-bomb movement also started to manifest itself. In Holland, however, a group of young people found its effects upon the establishment unsatisfactory, and opened fire on the holy consumer society itself.

A group of anarchism-inspired young people joined forces to set up 'Provo'. Their first acts of provocation won an immediate and negative response from the authorities. Robert Jasper Grootveld, the self-styled Smoke Magician, was carrying on a one-man guerilla campaign against the tobacco industry, and his well-publicized stunts greatly appealed to the Provos. Soon, weekly happenings were staged in the centre of Amsterdam. They would perform bizarre little plays, or deliver a sermon against the slavery of consumerism, and they soon started to draw large crowds. The poor, confused authorities could think of only one way to respond to the challenge: with the truncheon. The Provos believed in 'dropping out': this seemed scandalous to their parents, but it appealed greatly to students, schoolkids, working youths, artists and other hangers-on, mostly youngsters not yet integrated into the production process.

In the first issue of their paper, 'Provo', an article called 'Introduction to Provocative Thinking' outlined their critique of society:

'Why is Provo called Provo? Are we negative or positive? What is our norm? What are our tactics?

'Prov = Provo, because for us Provo is the only way left in our present society. To climb the social ladder, to hold a position in society, means active collaboration with capitalism and militarism: it means condoning the coming nuclear holocaust: it means surrendering to the myopic sop of TV. You could call us anti-professional. We can't think of any job which will not actively encourage and prolong the state of emergency under which we live. The worker produces junky products out of which the capitalist squeezes his profit; the civil servant administrates the victims of bureaucracy; the inventions of the scientists are violated for military ends.

'The antisocial Provo is the bright light at the end of the tunnel. His appearance is a spoke in the wheels of Progress, progress that thunders on, heedless of the bomb under the tracks, just ahead ...

'We preach provocation as *the* way to resist society: we hope the Provo will see that his job degrades him, that he is only a little fuse in the time-bomb which is society, and that he will dedicate himself to full-time provocation. We want to see Provos developing from rowdy hoodlums to anarchistic enemies of the state. Today, the Provo is usefully exercising his skills in provoking the fuzz, in friendly riots on the Dam, in throwing firecrackers through letter boxes. Tomorrow, the Provo will have to see the police as the real enemy, he will have to attack the royal palace on the Dam, and throw bombs through the letterbox of the BVD (Internal Security Service building).

'Because only they, the young, the rebellious and the idle, are still capable of action. They are ready for

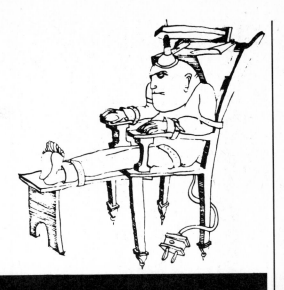

revolution, not the so-called working class, which is bound hand and foot and chained to the social system. The Provos are the last revolutionary class in the Netherlands (we include Teddy boys, beatniks and magicians among the Provos).

'We reject capitalism, bureaucracy, militarism and the inevitable political and military holocaust (World War III). We welcome resistance, freedom and creativity. In other words, we reject the positive and support the negative. We love hate and hate love. All we want is for everybody to fight the outside world in the name of their own existence.'

The Provo riots were a catalyst for the expression of all sorts of dissatisfaction, and opened up a creative field of combat between the authorities and the people. Politics and art were brought together in their happenings. The passive political spectator, the passive museum-visitor, was transformed into an active participant in the street.

As the movement grew its character changed. The total rejection of society as it was run eventually gave rise to new ideas on how it ought to be run. In retrospect the 'White Plans' produced by the Provos for changing society seem reformist, but at the time they were intended to be provocative. What they were really doing was exposing various kinds of oppression as experienced by members of the Provo movement. For example, the 'White Wives and White Children Plan' was one of the first post-war expressions of militant feminism; the 'White Chimneys Plan' was an outcry against pollution; the 'White Bike Plan' was a critique of public transport; and the 'White Houses Plan' a forerunner of the squatters movement.

The Provos were a living critique of the dull reality of everyday life, but they were by no means a homogeneous group. Eventually a split occurred which led to squabbling amongst the different groups of students, young workers and anarchists. When in June

Page from *Billy the Kid*, by Willem, Netherlands, 1968.
It's six o'clock in China, the day dawns, and the chaplain says a short morning prayer.
'Our President Who Art in the White House, Hallowed be Thy Name.
'Thy Kingdom come, Thy Will be done, in the Pentagon as well as in China.
'Give us this day our daily popcorn and give us our napalm, so that we can give napalm to those who trespass against us.
'And lead us not into ambushes and deliver us from the Yellow Peril.
'For Thine is the Democracy, the dollar and the Great Society for ever and ever.
'Amen.'
'Come on, soldier, time to get up.'

53

1966 the Amsterdam building workers clashed with their own trade unions, one of the Provo factions felt it had to distance itself from the riots. Had the divided Provos managed to agree to join forces with the rebellious workers, it would have meant a real threat to the power of the authorities. The movement was fizzling out, it was becoming paralysed and limited, and in the end it was decided by a self-appointed few to kill off the Provo image once and for all.

The Provo movement inspired one of today's best-known European political cartoonists, Willem. A number of the cartoons he drew for 'Provo' magazine led to legal prosecution. Before he left Holland to live in France, he published a number of strips in underground papers — 'De Witte Krant' (The White Newspaper), 'Aloha' and 'OM'.

---

waarom stemmen lastige Amsterdammers PROVO ?

het lieverdje :

Provo heeft een heel nieuwe opvatting over A'dam;het moet de eerste speelstad ter wereld worden,waar geen happening verboden is en ieder vrij is te zeggen wat hij wil. Ugge,ugge,ik ben blij dat provoos Witte Schoorstenenplan een einde aan de luchtverontreiniging zal maken. De provoos zijn tegen Mobil Oil,die onze lucht verpesten zal.

de dokwerker :

De provoos verzetten zich principieel en positief tegen de Autoriteiten.Hun Witte Fietsenplan is dé oplossing voor de verkeerschaos in de stad,d.w.z. het Centrum sluiten voor particuliere autoos en daarvoor in de plaats openbaar vervoer:gemeentelijke Witte Fietsen, gratis trams en elektrotaxies.

domela nieuwenhuis:

Als anarchist stem ik zeker op Provo.In de gemeenteraad zullen zij de autoriteiten controleren en iedereen op de hoogte houden wat er met A'dam gebeurt.Recht voor allen,woningen voor allen. Leve Provoos Witte Woningenplan...het paleis moet niet leeg staan,maar gebruikt worden als stadhuis.Weg met de nazaten van koning Gorilla.

omdat PROVO positieve plannen biedt

waarom stemmen ook AUTORITEITEN PROVO ?

burgemeester VAN HALL

De provoos hebben gelijk, "Van Hall moet met vakantie" Het is te gek mij maar te laten begaan, demonstraties verbiedend, de politie ongestoord te laten ranselen, arresteren en fouilleren. Wil een Wit Wijf met mij op vakantie? Ik vrees van niet, die witte wijven zijn zo goed voorgelicht op speciale provoconsultatieburoos voor vrouwen en meisjes.Daarom zijn ze ook zo wit.

kommissaris LAND-MAN

Met hun Witte Kippenplan zijn de provoos mijn beste kameraden. De blauwe diktatuur moet ophouden. De agent moet sociaal werker worden i.p.v. een rammende smeris. De politie moet zo snel mogelijk door de gemeenteraad gekontroleerd worden en ontwapend, vóórdat er doden vallen, zoals van Hall vreest.Mijn mannen in een wit uniform.

VAN HEUTSZ

Vorige keer heb ik op Koekoek gestemd, maar nu ga ik Provo stemmen.Ik moet nodig weg als toonbeeld van het nederlands militairisme en koloniale strijd. In deze militaristische tijd,die de hele mensheid bedreigt wil ik niet de trotse generaal spelen. Haal me a.u.b. weg provoos.Voorwaarts, mars,geef geen 8 maar 12 op 1 juni, stem PROVO!

Provo election pamphlet, Netherlands, 1966.

WHY do troublesome Amsterdammers vote PROVO?

The Lieverdje (a statue in Amsterdam which is used as a symbol of the Provo movement). Provo thinks Amsterdam should be the first fun-city of the world, where no happening is forbidden, and everyone is free to say what he wants. Cough, cough...I am glad the Provos' White Chimney Plan will end this air pollution. They are fighting Mobil Oil, who are fouling our air.

The dockworker

The Provos resist the authorities. Their White Plan is the solution to traffic congestion in Amsterdam, i.e. to close the centre to cars, to be replaced by public transport: municipal white bicycles, free trams and electric taxis.

Domela Nieuwenhuis (Grand old man of Dutch workers' movement)

As an anarchist, I shall certainly vote Provo. They will control the authorities in the town council and keep everyone informed about what is going on in Amsterdam. Rights for everybody, housing for everybody. Hooray for the Provo Housing plans... The Dam Palace shouldn't just stand empty, it should be used as a Town Hall. Death to the descendants of King Gorilla (King Willem II)...

WHY do the authorities also vote PROVO?

Mayor Van Hall

The Provos are right, 'Van Hall should take a holiday'. It's ridiculous to go on allowing me to ban demonstrations and give the police a free hand to search and arrest. Will any White Woman come with me on my hols? I'm afraid she won't, because those White Women are so well-informed by special Provo advice centres. That's why they remain so white!

Police Commissioner Land-Man

The Provos are my friends with their White Cops plan. There must be an end to the blue dictatorship. The cop must become a social worker instead of a mugging villain. The police must be taken in hand immediately by the council and disarmed before deaths result, as van Hall fears. My men in *white* uniform.

Van Heutsz (Army general in Dutch colonies)

Last time I voted for Koekoek, but now I intend to vote for Provo. It's about time I stopped representing Dutch militarism and colonial strife. I don't want to play the part of a proud general in these martial times. Please take me away, Provos. Forward, march, vote Provo on 1st June!

Facing page: Everyone who reads this is dying. Willem in the Dutch underground magazine *OM*, Netherlands, 1969.

1.   DEATH has always been a form of entertainment. The ancient Romans threw Christians to the lions, the Christians tied heretics to the stake. 2.   Yes, public executions were popular, inventive executioners were always thinking up new tricks. At the end of the eighteenth century the French King found it imperative to win favour by offering the people entertainment, and stimulated the invention of the GUILLOTINE. 3.   But the guillotine was a talent- and man-eating medium (just like the TV of today) which made no exception for the royal family and co-operated with the Revolution. 4.   The guillotine was not only the start of the French bourgeois revolution, but also of the industrial revolution of the nineteenth century. In the 1880s the industrialization of death reached a new climax: the first electric chair was built in New York. 5.   However, this rapidly-expanding, dynamic branch of industry needed more and more death sentences. It was most irritating that every victim had first to be sought out, arrested, tried, and only then, after a lot of inane bickering, amongst stupid jurists, finally to be condemned. We therefore decided to stop paying heed to the inefficient juridical roundabout. Progress cannot be held back. 6.   Well, yes, and the things we did then...I sometimes still think with tenderness on those days of the steam engine, Glenn Miller music and primitive raids, back when we had to drag the people out of their homes and hiding places to murder them. Well, the situation has now changed... 7.   Today we are so far advanced that it is no longer necessary to set foot outside your living room to be poisoned —you have opened your doors to poisonous and cancerous materials everywhere — in the artificial colouring in your margarine, in your toilet cleaner, in your sprayed fruit, in your cigarette, in your cosmetics, your baby powders, etc. —hey miss! even in the air you breathe... 8.   Besides, you, yes you who are reading this, are presently dying slowly but surely from poisoning! Hahaha...the end.

DE DOOD IS ALTIJD EEN VORM VAN AMUSEMENT GEWEEST.

de oude romeinen wierpen de christenen voor de leeuwen, de christenen zetten hun ketters op de brandstapel.

ja, openbare terechtstellingen waren populair, inventieve beulen bedachten steeds nieuwe variaties,

tot aan het eind van de achtiende eeuw de franse koning zich genood- zaakt zag de gunst van het volk te winnen. Hij deed dit door de mensen steeds meer Amusement te bieden. en stimuleerde de uitvinding van de **GUILLOTINE**

Maar de guillotine was, net als nu de TV, een talent- en mensenverslindend medium, dat zelfs het koninklijk huis niet ontzag en Revolutie in de hand werkte.

De guillotine was niet alleen het begin van de franse burgerlijke revolutie, maar ook de start van de industriële revolutie in de 19e eeuw.

In de 1880's vond de industrialisatie van de dood een voorlopig hoogtepunt in de bouw van de eerste elektriese stoel te New York.

Maar deze, zich steeds sneller ontwikkelende dinamiese tak van industrie kreeg behoefte aan steeds meer ter dood veroordeelden. Het was dan ook nogal omslachtig om iedereen die omgebracht moest worden eerst te laten opsporen, arresteren, verhoren en

dan eindelijk na veel gekibbel met stomme juristen ter dood te laten veroordelen. Daarom besloten we ons maar niets meer aan te trekken van de inefficiënte juridiese rompslomp en onze gang maar te gaan. De vooruitgang laat zich niet tegenhouden.

Ja en wat we toen allemaal deden... Soms denk ik nog wel eens vertederd terug aan de tijd van stoomlokomo- tieven, Glenn-Millermuziek en primitieve razzia's, toen we de mensen nog uit hun huizen en schuilplaats- en moesten sleuren om ze te vermoorden. Dat ligt nu wel even anders

Vandaag de dag zijn we zover gevorderd dat niemand meer de huiskamer hoeft te verlaten om zwaar ver- giftigd te worden. Vrijwel overal hebben we kanker- verwekkende stoffen en andere vergiften in gedaan.

in de kleurstof in uw margarine

in uw toilet- reiniger

in uw bespoten fruit

in uw sigaret

enzovoort

Juffrouw! Zelfs in de lucht die u inademt!

in uw kosmetika

in uw insekten- verdelgings- middel

in uw babypoeder

Trouwens. U die dit leest, bent op het ogen- blik bezig een lang- zame maar zekere Vergiftigings- Dood te sterven!

Einde

THE RETURN OF THE DURUTTI COLUMN

For many, the mad happenings of the Provos came as a bolt out of the blue. But not for everybody. The International Situationists (IS), a cosmopolitan group of artists, as early as 1958 had started to formulate a radical critique of Western culture as well as its avant-garde. From the very start they had predicted social revolt along Provo lines as well as race riots like those in the 1965 Watts ghetto. The Situationists understood this kind of outburst better than the traditional forces of the Left. By the mid-sixties, their ideas had started to provoke interest. At the beginning of 1966 a small group of students in Strasbourg made contact with the IS. Largely thanks to the apathy that reigned amongst the 16,000-strong student body at the University of Strasbourg, this little group managed to get itself elected onto the committee of the Students' Union. No sooner were they there than they started to use union funds for their own purposes. They founded a 'society for the rehabilitation of Marx and Ravachol', and fly-posted 'The Return of the Durutti Column'—a Marxist strip cartoon—all over the walls of the city. They called for the closing of the Students' Union and distributed, with the help of the IS, thousands of copies of a brochure which ridiculed the lives and loves of the students. It was sensational stuff, the local as well as the international press pounced on it with glee. This all happened at the beginning of term, and it took right-wing students, aided by the traditional Left, a full three weeks to oust the extremists. The counter-attack was rounded off by the verdict of the local magistrate on 14 December:

'The accused have not denied the charge that they have misused student union funds. They openly confess that they paid 5,000 francs of the union's money to print 10,000 pamphlets, not to mention the cost of other IS-inspired literature.

'Without hesitation, without any moral scruples, these cynics have preached theft, vandalism, the abolition of work, total subversion and universal proletarian revolution; their only aim is unlimited pleasure.

'The wide distribution of this propaganda not only among the student population but also the general newspaper-reading public constitutes a threat to the morale, the reputation, the future of the Strasbourg students.'

The Strasbourg students' pamphlet is still published in different languages to this day, and the Strasbourg University scandal was a taste of things to come — the student revolt of 1968.

Facing page: Part of the comic that was distributed by 'the friends of Marx and Ravachol' in sleepy Strasbourg, France, 1966.
1. What has shocked them most was, not that things were as bad as they were to the point of petrification, but that others frivolously supposed that they would refrain from reacting violently to this situation. 2. That day they were once more playing out their lives in a great game of chance... 'What if we took over the National Union of Students?' 'Well. I suppose it would be fun, but I think we'd be pretty bored among the trade-unionist rabble!' 'We might as well attend Abraham Mole's lectures without laughing!' 'Besides we don't have students' union cards.' 3. 'Why don't we nick some?' 4. By stealing goods to give them away again, certain teddy boys returned to, and improved upon, the primitive custom of giving which existed in archaic societies. This practice of giving was ruined by the ensuing practice of exchange based on formalization of social relations, which assumed a low level of production. Thus they are better adapted to a society which defines itself as a welfare society because they go beyond it. 5. In such a society, the attraction of theft pushes the most timid people into unthinkable and impossible areas. Life becomes a game, the game becomes life. They need to find, in all kinds of ways, new ground for experiment, new powers, to fight effectively against this power-based society. 6. 'How can we laugh without being heard?' 'We have covered ourselves by making sure that we have the hatred of all the old guard militants and all the old political forces.'
7. 'Two thousand years of Christianity have developed the masochism of the intellectuals: this is our chance, and not only here.'

LE RETOUR DE LA COLONNE DURUTTI

Situationist strip from Sweden, 1970.

Live Life

1. 'The goal of a revolutionary movement is the abolition of all classes...'
2. 'Without creating a new class at the same time.' 3. 'All power to the workers' councils—not to the Party!' 4. 'Dammit, that itches.' 5. 'We must develop a critique of life as a whole, not just the socio-economic power structure.' 6. 'We don't want to manage the world. We must change it.' 'Great, I'll join you.' 7. 'So-called revolutionary ideology is just an attempt to stop the revolution.' 8. 'I'm not sacrificing my life for a bunch of filthy power-specialists and bureaucrats.' 9. 'Umm!...Where was I?...Marx's ideas are really a critique of our everyday lives.' 'Out with all bosses. Oooh!' Council for the destruction of the State.

How New Zealand Situationists treated a Dubonnet advertisement, New Zealand, 1972. © *Cock*.

Facing page: Poster by the Internationale Situationniste, France, 1966.

1. In our spectacular society where all you can see is things and their price... 'There's nothing they won't do to raise the standard of boredom.' 2. The only free choice is the refusal to pay. 'Have a sweater! I've nicked three. What did you get?' 'Two old books and a bottle of gin.' 3. All energy wasted on half measures strengthens the grip of the old regime. 'How right you are to steal books. Culture is everybody's birthright.' 'Culture? Ug! The ideal commodity — the one which helps all the others. No wonder you want us all to go for it!' 'How interesting. Do come and talk about it on Sunday at the Centre for Contemporary Culture.' 'Look out! It's the fuzz!' 'A fucking priest more like.' No matter how radical the gesture, ideology tries to recuperate it. 4. But total oppression creates a language of total dissent. 'That was a close shave!' 'How about a movie?' 'No, there's only a Godard on and he's just another fucking preacher. C'mon girls, let's go to my place.' 5. And the restrictions imposed on pleasure make the dream of living for pleasure even more attractive. 'Oh well, I suppose it's back to the grindstone.' 'Slave labour you mean.' 'Back to all the cons. Back to the family.' 6. Don't put up with partial demands. 'You make it, you own it.' 'Don't change bosses. Change Life!' 'Workers Control!' 'Death to the rulers!' 'Let's run things ourselves!'

Comrades, this is only the beginning. If you want to know more about yourselves and your possibilities, read Internationale Situationniste. Issue no. 11 is just out. Postbox 30703 Paris.

Comic by the Italian section of the International Situationists, Italy, 1969.
1. 'What will become of the totality inherent in the unitarian society when it is confronted with the subverting of this unity by the bourgeoisie?'
2. 'Would an illusory reconstruction of this unity succeed in confusing the worker alienated by consumerism?' 3. 'But what will become of the totality in such a contradictory society?' 4. 'How can we supersede this society and all of its superficial organizations and still expect a happy ending?' 'This is something you should know and it will be revealed in the second part of this study.'

Facing page: Belgian Situationists added a new meaning to a cartoon by Willem, Belgium, 1973.
How long are we going to let them jiggle our balls, comrades?
1. When you're born the first thing you face is aggression — a slap on the bum. 2. Then they stick you behind bars. ('Stop sucking your thumb!') 3. Tyranny rules. ('God's watching you!' 'Hands above the blankets, filthy beast!') 4. They make you eat shit. ('Eat it all up!') 5. They stuff you into silly clothes 6. and pack you off to school ('We're rid of him.' 'One day he'll thank us!') 7. where you're finally broken in. 9. They turn you into consumer durables ('At last they look human!') 10. and force you to compete with each other. ('At your service, Sir.' 'Well done teacher.') 11. Rebellion is badly organized. 12. Some practise passive resistance ('What, failed again?' 'Parent = cop.') 13. or escape. 14. But the tyrants always have the upper hand. ('Are you still a virgin?' 'What will the neighbours think?') 15. Because the majority capitulate and collaborate ('OK, you're hired.') 16. and end up supporting them! ('Just like his old man!' 'Now it's my turn!')
Comrades! Break the vicious circle of authority! Stop giving orders! Stop taking orders! Stop giving in!!!!
Bureau for the decolonization of everyday life.

THE INTERNATIONAL CONSPIRACY

The International Situationists at first directed their criticism at the avant-garde in art, but soon saw a conflict with society as a whole, a society which creates the conditions for the need for an avant-garde. Out of their desire to free the creativity that exists in each of us, they initiated a psychological attack on the system: the system which represses creativity and reduces us to passive slaves of an artificial world full of false desires and needs (the 'spectacle'). They saw the violent protest of the Teddy boys, the Provos and the Watts ghetto blacks as a sign of a new revolutionary consciousness. The following article, which first appeared in their paper, the 'International Situationist', about the Watts riots, was later reprinted as a brochure entitled 'The Rise and Fall of the Spectacular Commodity Economy':

'The blacks are not isolated in their struggle because a *new proletarian consciousness*—the consciousness of not being the master of one's activity, of one's life, in the slightest degree—is taking form in America amongst strata whose refusal of modern capitalism resembles that of the negroes. Indeed, the first phase of the negro struggle has been the signal to a movement of opposition which is spreading. In December 1964 the students of Berkeley, frustrated in their participation in the civil rights movement, ended up by calling a strike to oppose the system of California's "multiversity", and by extension the social system of the US, in which they are allotted such a passive role. Immediately, drinking and drug orgies were uncovered among the students — the same supposed activities for which the negroes have long been castigated. This generation of students has since invented a new form of struggle against the dominant spectacle, the teach-in, a form taken up by the Edinburgh students on October 20th a propos of the Rhodesian crisis. This clearly imperfect and primitive type of opposition represents the stage of discussion which refuses to be limited in time (academically), and in this its logical outcome is a progression to practical activity. Also in October, thousands of demonstrators appeared in the streets of Berkeley and New York, their cries echoing those of the Watts rioters: "Get out of our district and out of Vietnam!" The whites, becoming more radical, have stepped outside the law: "courses" are given on how to defraud the recruiting boards, draft cards are burnt and the act televised. In the affluent society, disgust for affluence and for its price is finding expression. The spectacle is being spat on by an advanced sector whose autonomous activity denies its values.'

Here is what the IS founding members saw as their most important task: 'We must present everywhere a revolutionary alternative to the dominant culture; we must co-ordinate all investigations presently being carried out without an overall perspective; to encourage the most progressive artists and intellectuals, by means of criticism and propaganda, to join forces with us.'

The first issue of the 'International Situationist' appeared in 1958. In it, they dismissed the whole of our culture, from town planning to the Beat generation: the whole political spectrum was relegated to the rubbish tip: 'We must go further, much further, than the surrealists. Why? Because we don't want to die of boredom. Degenerating surrealists, misinformed youths, angry young men, teenage rebels; they may not understand what forces drive them, but they have this in common: they all have a goal, and they are all bored. Our modern age has already condemned itself. We, the situationists, are left to carry out the sentence.'

The Situationists were the first politically motivated group to make use of photographs with 'balloons', and to adapt the texts of existing comic strips. They called this technique 'detournement' (diversion), and defined it as follows: ' "Diversion" is the recycling of existing artistic elements in a new context which lends them a totally new meaning.' This idea was not a new one in artistic thought, but the Situationists adopted it because they recognized the value of the comic strip as a mass medium.

One of the IS's most active members, Deen J.V. Martin, was soon prosecuted for publishing 'subversive strips'. In 1964 he first got into trouble with the police on the occasion of a Danish princess marrying the Greek crown prince: he issued a picture of Christine Keeler with the following caption: 'I agree with the IS: it is more honourable to be a prostitute like me than to be the spouse of Constantine the fascist.' The next year,

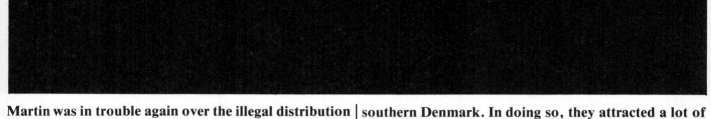

Martin was in trouble again over the illegal distribution of IS cartoons in Spain. The Danish branch of Moral Rearmament also brought charges against him. Martin in turn declared the IS's opposition to all the values for which Moral Rearmament stood, and announced the IS would be actively engaged in moral disarmament. The case was dismissed.

Apart from the events in Strasbourg, the IS were also involved in large-scale demonstrations in Denmark when the German army embarked on manoeuvres in southern Denmark. In doing so, they attracted a lot of publicity, which helped to spread their propaganda.

In the years that followed, groups appeared in many countries all over the world expressing the wish to ally themselves with the IS. Their ideas were translated and spread as far as Japan, South Africa and New Zealand, and were inevitably accompanied by the famous photo-strip montages.

One of the posters taken down by the strike committee at the LSE sit-in, England, 1968.

Welcome back to the superheroes, in *Archduke,* a small avant-garde magazine, England, 1968. © *Archduke.*

65

this poster is for flyposting

Situationist strip-poster by a group called Catalyst, England, 1971. © *Mole Express.*   Facing page: Situationists strip on the cover of *International Times.*

it
The International Times

No. 26   LONDON 1/6 ENGLAND   FEB 16-29, 1968

IN OUR SPECTAC-ULAR SOCIETY WHERE ALL YOU CAN SEE IS THINGS AND THEIR PRICE...

THERE'S NOTHING THEY WON'T DO TO RAISE THE STANDARD OF BOREDOM

THE ONLY FREE CHOICE IS THE REF-USAL TO PAY

HALF A DRESS — I'VE NICKED THREE WHAT DO YOU GET?

Please come again

PHILOSOPHY, IN THE BOUDOIR AND A PINT OF GIN

IDEOLOGY TRIES TO INTEGRATE EVEN THE MOST RADICAL ACTS

HOW RIGHT YOU ARE TO STEAL BOOKS! CULTURE IS EVERY-BODY'S BIRTHRIGHT

CULTURE? UGH! THE IDEAL COMMODITY — THE ONE WHICH HELPS SELL ALL THE OTHERS! NO WONDER YOU WANT US ALL TO GO FOR IT!

MAYBE YOU CAN GET THE HIPPIES, BABY, BUT YOU CAN'T GET ME

HOW INTERESTING! DO COME AND TALK ABOUT IT NEXT SUNDAY AT THE ROUNDHOUSE

LOOK OUT, IT'S THE FUZZ!

A PSYCHIATRIST, MORE LIKE!

ALL ENERGY WASTED ON HALF MEASURES STRENGTHENS THE TYRANNICAL GRIP OF THE OLD REGIME

BUT TOTAL REPRESSION CREATES A LANGUAGE OF TOTAL DISSENT

BAR

NO THERE'S ONLY A COMMIE ON AND HE'S JUST ANOTHER BLOODY BEATLE — C'MON LET'S GO BACK TO MY PLACE

'BETTER THAT THE WHOLE WORLD SHOULD BE DESTROYED AND PERISH UTTERLY THAN THAT A FREE MAN SHOULD REFRAIN FROM ONE ACT TO WHICH HIS NATURE MOVES HIM'   (K. MARX)

SLAVE LABOUR YOU MEAN

BACK TO ALL THE CONS, BACK TO THE F—ING FAMILY

OH WELL, I SUPPOSE I'D BETTER GO TO THE COMMUNE

BURN, BABY, BURN!

NIHILISTS! ONE MORE EFFORT IF YOU WANT TO BE REVOLUTIONARIES!

WHATEVER THE EYE SEES AND COVETS, LET THE HAND GRASP IT!

REMEMBER REMEMBER THE FIFTH OF NOVEMBER!

LET'S GET THEM!

WORKERS' CONTROL!

WILDCAT COMICS

IN THE SOCIETY OF THE SPECTACLE A BUREAUCRA-TIC CLASS ACQUIRES POWER IN THE NAME OF RATIONALITY, WHILE THE BOURGEOISIE, CONFIDENT THAT ITS PROJECT, THE DEVELOPMENT OF THE COMMODITY ECONOMY, IS BEING MAINTAINED, RE-TIRES TO THE WINGS. THE UNIONS BECOME INSTRU-MENTS OF THE RULING CLASS, PART OF THE BUR-EAUCRATIC MACHINE.

WHEN WILDCATS AND SABOTAGE REVEAL THE IRRATIONALITY OF THE BUREAUCRACY IN RELA-TION TO HUMAN DE-SIRES, ANTI-BUREAUCRATS, POLITICIANS OF PARTICI-PATION, ARRIVE TO JUSTI-FY THE MAINTENANCE OF HIERARCHICAL POWER BY REDISCOVERING THE PROBLEM OF SURVIVAL. IN THE FACE OF FANTASTIC ACCUMULATION OF MA-TERIAL POSSIBILITIES, THEY ENCOURAGE THE PRO-LETARIAT TO BARGAIN FOR THE PIECEMEAL MANAGEMENT OF ITS SURVIVAL, SO THAT IT WON'T CONSTRUCT FOR ITSELF THE RICH LIFE NOW POSSIBLE.

THE SAN FRANCISCO CABLE CAR WILDCAT OF 1970 BEGAN WHEN A SPONTAN-EOUS DEM-OCRATIC ASSEMBLY OF DRIVERS

Ostr. Juli 1971

68 This, and following three pages: Situationist intervention in a San Francisco wildcat strike of cable-car drivers, USA, 1971.

DECIDED TO RETURN HER CALLS TO THE BARN.

THEIR AUTONOMOUS ACTION, THOUGH IN RESPONSE TO A PARTICULAR INJUSTICE

SPLAT

EXPRESSED A PRACTICAL CRITIQUE OF THE TOTAL INJUSTICE OF HIERARCHICAL POWER

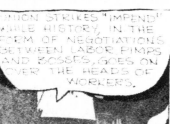

UNION STRIKES "IMPEND" WHILE HISTORY, IN THE FORM OF NEGOTIATIONS BETWEEN LABOR PIMPS AND BOSSES, GOES ON OVER THE HEADS OF WORKERS.

ON THE OTHER HAND,

A WILD-CAT COMES OUT OF "NOWHERE"

JUST BECAUSE WORKERS THEMSELVES TAKE POWER IN THEIR OWN HANDS

THROUGH "COMMUNITY CONTROL OF MUNI-FARES" WE HOPE TO GIVE EVERYONE IN SAN FRANCISCO THE OPPORTUNITY TO PARTICIPATE IN THE MANAGEMENT OF THE MOST BANAL PARTICULAR OF THEIR EVERYDAY MISERY.

BUT BECAUSE WE NEVER DID GRASP THE SIGNIFICANCE OF OUR ACTION, OUR DIALOGUE BECAME TRAPPED IN POWER'S LANGUAGE. THE PASSION OF TOTAL REFUSAL WAS REDUCED TO THE BOREDOM OF NEGOTIATING ISSUES.

AT EACH LEVEL OF THE HIERARCHY, EVERY TIME WE LET SOMEONE REPRESENT US OR TOOK OUR CASE TO AN AUTHORITY (STEWARDS, UNION OFFICIALS, MAYOR) OUR GAME WAS FURTHER REDUCED TO QUANTITATIVE PARTICULARS.

WE AT THE MUNI-DRIVERS ASSOCIATION CONTINUE THE LOGIC OF THE FAILURE OF OUR WILDCAT BY APPEALING TO YET ANOTHER AUTHORITY—THIS TIME AN ABSTRACTION—THE "COMMUNITY" WE'VE BECOME BOYSCOUTS COMPETING FOR MERIT BADGES OF "PUBLIC SERVICE"

P.O. BOX 1044 BERKELEY CA.

comrades, it's your turn to play!

communications to:
point–blank!
p.o. box 2233
station A
berkeley, cal

Situationist comic based on staff magazine, *AT&T Express*, USA, 1971.

the sexuality of dialectics

Situationist comic directed at Women's Lib, USA, 1971.

INITIATION RITES FOR STUDENTS

1. ORIENTATION: CONTENT OF THE EDUCATION

a) THE LIE

PROFESSOR of THEORY

University education begins with Freedom, Democracy, Free Enterprise, the official MYTH which covers up the bureaucratic CORPORATE and MILITARY REALITY.

MILITARY requirements of the System: ARMED DEFENSE.

PROFESSOR of APPLIED SCIENCE

b) THE BUREAUCRACY

University education continues by teaching the student to accept authority and obey orders. He is taught to manipulate others without being conscious that he is manipulated.

CORPORATE requirements of the System: PRODUCTION and CONSUMPTION.

PROFESSOR of APPLIED SCIENCE

University education ADJUSTS the student for a corporate job by giving him a FRAGMENTED VIEW OF HIS SOCIAL SITUATION (Enough to make him produce and consume, but not enough to arouse revolutionary consciousness).

2. THE FUNCTION OF THE CAPITALIST UNIVERSITY

a) STUNTING

SPECTACLE   STUDENT

The student whose energy has not yet been killed by elementary and high school education will want to DECIDE, to ACT, to CREATE. The University STOPS HIM. He is taught that the social system is NATURAL and ETERNAL, and that he is IMPOTENT.

b) MAIMING

SPECTATOR

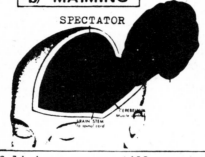

If living energy still remains, IT IS REMOVED. The student is reduced to a SPECTATOR. He is not given THE ABILITY TO DEFINE HIMSELF AS A CONSCIOUS AGENT WHOSE SOCIAL ACTIVITY CAN OVERTHROW THE CORPORATE-MILITARY SYSTEM.

c) HOUSEBREAKING

ROBOT

The student is stunted and maimed, BUT NOT DESTROYED; housebroken, but not broken. Once he learns his place, he is TRAINED and PROGRAMED to serve the system without questioning it.

3. THE MEANS

a) INTIMIDATION

If the student is tempted to attack the bureaucracy or question the myth, he is intimidated by the ENORMITY of the institution and by the infinite mass of measured DETAILS poured on him by "objective" and "neutral" PROFESSORS.

b) AUTHORITY

Once he understands that decision and creative social action are ABOVE HIS REACH, the student is ready for graduation. He understands the basic lesson of the University: SUBMISSION TO AUTHORITY.

c) CONTROL

University professors and administrators ENFORCE CORRECT LEARNING by means of TESTS AND GRADES; they reinforce it with the threat of military induction. When this control system breaks down, clubs, gas and lethal weapons are used.

Situationist pamphlet distributed in California High Schools, USA, 1971.

INITIATION RITES FOR PROFESSORS AND ADMINISTRATORS

When students refuse to be had, bizarre events begin to occur:

CONFRONTATION

THE STUDENT QUESTIONS

To understand his situation, the student throws out the American MYTH as an explanation of his reality, and rejects the GRADE as a limitation on his thought or action.

THE STUDENT ATTACKS

Freed from the carrots and sticks of the academic bureaucracy, THE STUDENT no longer submits. THE END OF THE STUDENT'S SUBMISSION IS THE END OF THE PROFESSOR'S AUTHORITY. The student no longer adjusts, HE ACTS!

THE STUDENT EXPOSES

The student exposes the SPECTACLE. He unveils the obvious: The Corporate-Military System is neither natural nor eternal; it is created by human practice and can be destroyed by revolutionary practice.

ACTION

INDIVIDUAL ACTION

Rejecting the MYTH as well as the BUREAUCRACY, the student becomes CONSCIOUS OF HIS SOCIAL POWER and thus DANGEROUS TO THE SYSTEM; if he lets himself be isolated, he'll be destroyed.

SOCIAL ACTION

By exposing the ideological content of classroom lectures, by communicating with other students through posters on walls, through critical discussions and leaflets, STUDENTS BEGIN TO CHANGE THEIR SITUATION.

REVOLUTIONARY ACTION

When students cease to be passive observers, THE SPECTACLE IS SHATTERED. Students become conscious social agents: REVOLUTIONARIES.

ESCALATION

Conscious of their power, students begin to struggle--and are repressed, not by the University, but by the CONCENTRATED POWER OF THE CORPORATE-MILITARY SYSTEM.

The repressive power of the system rests on the sold labor of working populations. Used, intimidated and powerless, reduced to factors, spectators and objects, these populations are potential revolutionaries.

The power of CAPITAL will end WHEN WORKERS CEASE TO SELL THEIR LABOR. The students' struggle cannot be limited to the University, because the liberation of the world's working population is the condition for the liberation of students.

Situationist pamphlet distributed in California High Schools, USA, 1971.

The experience of the proletarian revolutions of the past (Russia 1905, Kronstadt 1921, Spain 1936) has shown that direct democracy can only be achieved through the absolute power of workers' councils — democratic assemblies who elect members as delegates to co-ordinate and perform various tasks...

(Durruti Column: armed workers' militia, Spain, 1936)

We aim at the creation of a situation where man does not reproduce himself in any given form, but produces his totality; where he does not seek to remain something formed by the past...

But is in the absolute movement of becoming!

Revolution is nothing less than an armed critique of society. The first step in this is the seizure of the vital terrain of the enemy (means of production, schools, etc.) with an aim towards its complete transformation. Just like in France, 1968, the revolutionaries in schools must link up with revolutionaries in other areas of society in a common struggle against capitalism.

(Revolutionaries making Molotov cocktails: Paris 1968)

The movement for a new world must destroy anybody who seeks to represent it!

We won't let all the bureaucrats recuperate the struggle and return it to all the old shit of the past - sacrifice, leaders, etc.

Meanwhile, inside the school conference room, we find---

And we'll let the blacks control the third world studies program

Hey! come back! don't you support us and self-determination like the BSU does?

C'mon son - do it like Huey P. Newton says - aren't you for community control?

Fuck off, bastards! I won't take part in your con game!

Long live Watts! Screw Huey!

Man only plays when he is a man in the full meaning of the word, and he is fully human only when he plays!

The urge to destroy is really a creative urge!

PLAYING WITH RIFLED CASH REGISTER
WATTS 1965

Since high school is just one lie in a society based on lies, the project which aims at the end of high school must fight capitalism in all its forms.

It must understand the radicalism of a wildcat strike as well as a classroom disruption!

This radicalism has nothing to do with the Maoist creeps who drool about the need for schools to "serve the people." All forms of false opposition, like the New Left which seeks to replace the existing hierarchy with a "revolutionary" one, only support the present order of domination.

Oh! no! not her! With her sense of duty and sacrifice she might as well be a Catholic!

Hi, Wally--

What time will you PICK ME UP tonight?

You asked to take me to the PEACE RALLY-- remember?

Why should I waste my time going to one of your feeble, guilt-ridden circuses.

What? You mean you don't support the NLF?

Sorry... I don't choose between bureaucrats!

We fight for ourselves or we don't fight at all!

SENIOR HIGH SCHOOL REPORT CARD

NAME				SCHOOL		GRADE	STUDENT NO.	QUARTER	DATE
QUARTER GRADE 1 OR 3	2 OR 4	SEM CD	PER	Courses of action			FACTORS INFLUENCING GRADE		
							FAVORABLE		UNFAVORABLE
				SABOTAGE COMPUTER CENTERS					
				PRINT UP PHONY REPORT CARDS					
				DESTROY DISCIPLINARY FILES					
				PRINT FAKE ANNOUNCEMENTS					
				SEIZE THE PUBLIC ADDRESS SYSTEM					

THE GAME BEGINS

From boredom can arise at any time the irresistible refusal of uniformity and authority. The revolutionary takes his desires for reality because he believes in the reality of his desires

THE FREE SPEECH MOVEMENT

Student protest in America gave its first sign of life in the Free Speech Movement, founded at the University of Berkeley in 1964. It was triggered off by the Board's decision to declare the campus entrance out of bounds to distribution of political propaganda. San Francisco's Bay Area—including Berkeley—was at that time second only to New York in raising volunteers for the civil rights drive in the deep South. So it didn't take much to make the students stand up for their rights on their own territory. They decided simply to ignore the authorities' ruling. On 1 October a student was arrested. His friends tried to intervene when police hustled him into a police car, but were beaten off with truncheons. This episode gave rise to a long series of confrontations between students and the authorities—who called in the cops. It was the first time a university had resorted to the law to put an end to an on-campus conflict. In an equally new development, the students staged a sit-in and decided to go on strike. As they had warned the authorities, 'the machine came to a grinding halt'.

A year later the conflict flared up again when the SDS (Students for a Democratic Society) organized protests against the recruiting of reserve Marine officers on campus. This kind of recruitment at universities was not unusual, but criticism of America's involvement in the war in Vietnam led to a new resistance to such practices. Over a thousand students participated in the strike and sit-in that followed. Some members of the staff expressed their solidarity with the students. The strike ended in a stalemate, although a gesture was made to give in to the students' least important demands. The new ground for further conflict remained.

A new bond arose between the previously isolated groups of hippies and more politically motivated activists. The older generation and the establishment began to feel threatened by this rejection of their traditional values, and the news media blew up this 'generation gap' to extreme proportions, concentrating on the extremist groups, while ignoring the other gaps in society — economic and social. The ever-increasing number of wildcat strikes among factory workers was relegated to the bottom of page three; meanwhile, the Hell's Angels were depicted as the devil incarnate, the Minutemen were extreme rightists, while the hippies, student radicals and Black Panthers were all written off as left-wing extremists. In a bid to formulate a radical critique of the so-called Great Society, the group 'Black Mask', which made its debut in New York in 1966, exposed the absurdity of the situation. According to them, these publicity-drawing opposition groups operated only in a restricted area which was allocated to them by the system. Other groups were developing along similar lines, notably the Resurgence Youth Movement and the Rebel Worker. In England, in the same year, a paper appeared which followed the same ideological trends: 'Heatwave'. These groups represented the most radical aspects of the youth movement, and not only in their critique of society: the protest movement itself was their main target. Typical of their reasoning is the following extract from the second issue of 'Heatwave':

'We are living through the break-up of an entire civilization. Contemporary society has only one foundation — its own inertia: the last vestiges of religion and ideology cannot conceal the extent of our mass-alienation. Nothing means anything any more. There seems to be no escape from the isolation and senselessness of our lives. For all of us the abyss seems likely to open at any moment. We are all alone in a world that has become one huge mad-house.

'Nowhere is there an adequate explanation of what it is we go through every day. The traditional revolutionary movement, to which desperate people might once have turned, has long since been integrated in the status quo and is no longer distinct from the rest of the bureaucratic machine. At best it is simply the vanguard of bureaucratic efficiency-reform. Nowhere does there exist a theoretical and analytical basis from which the increasingly unbearable contradictions of our daily life can be examined, attacked and destroyed: a basis exposing our modern poverty and revealing our possible wealth.

'...Over the last decade, *a new revolt* has begun to break in all the highly industrialized countries of the world, a revolt associated particularly closely with both the wildcat strikes and with the attitudes of contemporary rebel youth. This revolt is now out in the open: agitators and saboteurs are on the streets. The whole of official society (cops and psychiatrists, artists and sociologists, anarchists and architects) has tried to suppress, distort and re-integrate the phenomena of this, their crisis.

'... The first thing to be criticized is the crock of shit passed off as criticism. Opposition has degenerated into a series of disparate and fragmentary protests—against nuclear war, against colonialism and racial discrimination, against urban chaos, etc.— lacking any grip on the whole of modern society and presenting no serious challenge to the dominant set-up. *What should be criticized is, on the contrary, our normal everyday experience of life.* It is this that is so boring, disgusting and senseless.

'... We reject the *whole* system of work and leisure, of production and consumption, to which life has been reduced by bureaucratic capitalism.

'Put in different terms: it is the concept of "total revolution" which has been lost. It has degenerated into a theory of the rectification of economic and political structures, whereas all the most radical periods of the past revolutionary movement were animated by the desire *to transform the whole nature* of human experience, to create a world in which the desires of each individual could be realized, without restriction. The only real problem is how to live life to the full.'

The people who produced 'Heatwave' later set up a group called King Mob, which associated itself for a short time with the Situationists. 'Heatwave' first introduced in England the use of superheroes to voice political ideologies. Their example was followed enthusiastically. King Mob published a number of issues of a paper of the same name, some posters featuring comic characters and a poster-format comic strip called 'Smashit'. During the sit-in at the London School of Economics in 1968, their posters and cartoons were stripped off the walls by the strike committee. Though they soon vanished from the political scene, King Mob influenced a lot of people, and Situationist comic strips contined to turn up in all kinds of alternative papers, including 'Mole Express'.

In the States, Black Mask, after publishing about ten issues of their own paper, dissolved into a number of splinter groups, some of whom became involved with the Motherfuckers, while a few others founded an American limb of the International Situationists. Both in New York and in California Situationist groups were making their presence felt, and much use was made of the now well-tried formula of photo-montage strips. Contradiction, a Californian group, for example, produced in 1971 a large poster called 'Bureaucratic Comic'. An attempt was made to intervene in current wildcat strikes. 'Wildcat Comix' was published for the benefit and instruction of San Francisco's cable-car drivers, and during a nationwide wildcat strike of the

AT&T telephone company workers, Contradiction joined forces with the Point Blank group to publish a facsimile of the AT&T house newspaper, in which the revolutionary possibilities of the strike were emphasized. In response to the confrontations in the universities, Point Blank also published a comic book that contained a radical analysis of the whole educational system and praised the reformist power of the student movement. The women's movement received similar attention.

The Situationist pamphlet about the scandal at Strasbourg University had already been published in translation in New York in 1968, and since then the photo-montage method for comic strips has been widely adopted outside the IS in underground and radical student papers. Strips like 'The Adventures of Fred Philmore', 'Defecation in Deuteronomy', 'The Era of Harmony', 'The Romance' and 'The Point of No Return' demonstrate that not only were the Situationists' practical techniques adopted, but also that something of their radical critique of the consumer society had filtered through to the political conscious-ness of the 'movement'. It is sometimes funny to see, in some of these underground papers — the 'Berkeley Barb', 'Helix', 'Good Times' etc. — how Situationist texts attacking all kinds of leftist groups and vanguard ideologies appeared quite happily next to solemn por-traits of Mao, Castro and Ho Chi Min. The use of the montage principle was particularly popular in the propaganda of anarchist and council Communist groups, who shared much of the Situationists' critique.

Incidentally, a popular sport was launched, which owed something to the montage principle, though nothing to comics: spray-painting slogans on highway billboards.

The Motherfuckers set themselves up as champions of the new lifestyle which had been developed on the Lower East Side, New York's hippy ghetto. Under their direction, about four hundred 'flower congs' stormed New York's Museum of Modern Art at the time of a Dada exhibition. They also staged numerous attacks on the rock-and-roll palace Fillmore East, demanding that at least one evening per week be reserved there for community activities. During the sit-in at Columbia they made the suggestion that the university's priceless collection of rare ceramics be placed behind the barricades. But perhaps the most important thing about the Motherfuckers was that they used a new language—a colloquial, everyday language—and took a stand against the worn-out jargon of intellectual activists.

Similar groups were formed in other large American cities in 1968 and 1969. They represented a pure but desperate radical adventurism, which ended with the arrest of their most active members. They were the first to emphasize the need for small guerrilla groups that would live as collectives and would be united under a loose federalist umbrella. Though the Motherfuckers themselves soon disappeared, their tactics were taken over by the SDS and Weathermen. Contributors to the Motherfuckers' newspaper, 'Rat', which was crammed with political manifestos, were first-rate artists like Bobby London, J. Schenkman and Frank Adams.

'Deuteronomium', USA, 1968. © Rat.

THE ROMANCE

BOB MAiER

The Romance, USA, 1969, in a radical student paper.
© *Kalamazoo Proper.*

REALLY REVOLTING!
HIGH AT P T&T

SEE PAGE

Situationist comic on the cover of the *Berkeley Barb*, USA, 1968.

To create at long last

a situation that goes beyond

the point of no return

— 7 —

Situationist-influenced strip, USA, 1969. © *Dock of the Bay.*

GUERILLA BILLBOARD ART

Spray-gun graffiti in the Bay Area, USA, 1970.
Facing page: The Adventures of Fred Philmore, USA, 1970.
© *Berkeley Barb.*

Motherfucker Manifesto, USA, 1968. © *Rat.*

From the Book of the Motherfucker

Motherfucker comic, USA, 1968. © *Rat.*

Facing page: Motherfucker manifesto, USA, drawn by Spain, USA, 1960. © *Rat.*

A.C.I.D. = Action Committee for
Immediate Defense

For Information:
Check out Leaflets, Motherfuckers,
Common Ground Coffee-house, Free
Fillmore (Wed.), and all other Lib-
erated Spaces on the Lower East Side.

A.C.I.D. needs You for the protection
of your Community...

ACID is community patrol to prevent harassment from the Pig. ACID is Bail Fund, Legal help,
and Self-Defense classes. ACID is the Lower East Side Hip Community's response to the possibility of defending and creating the Power to Survive, to Struggle, and to Win. If you
can help with desperately needed Bail Money send to: A.C.I.D., Box 512, Cooper Station, N.Y.,N.Y.

THE FREE PRESS

The first European member of the Underground Press Syndicate was 'Peace News', the mouthpiece of the British ban-the-bomb movement. Here as in other Western countries the peace movement was the springboard for the youth revolution. A new generation took over in organizations like the Committee for Nuclear Disarmament, Direct Action Committee, Spies for Peace and the Committee of One Hundred. After the launching of 'International Times' (IT) in London in 1967, a whole range of underground newspapers appeared. To name but a few: 'The Hustler', 'Hapt', 'Oz', 'Black Dwarf'; in Holland, the 'Witte Krant', 'Psy-In', 'Real Free Press', 'Om'; in Switzerland, 'Hotcha'; in Germany, 'Radikalinski' and 'Linkeck'; in Belgium, 'Den Uyl'; in Sweden, 'Puss'; and in Denmark 'Superlove'. The flood of papers and pamphlets proved the youth revolt to be a world-wide movement with its own news media.

Although almost every publication that attached itself to the UPS represented different backgrounds, ideologies and goals, they were all united on one front: protest against the Vietnam War. While it was a central theme in some papers like the 'Berkeley Barb', however, it was only peripheral in papers like the 'San Francisco Oracle', which represented quite another facet of the movement. The 'Oracle's' editors considered themselves spokesmen for a spiritual movement and the inner revolution: meditation, LSD and macrobiotics. The 'Oracle' made a number of breakthroughs in graphic design, and their experiments with new techniques were influential.

The violent uprising and equally violent suppression of Detroit's Black ghettos in 1967 hardly affected the 'love generation', but had a great impact on the more politicized groups and papers. The Black Panther Party had been going for about one year, and had a great following in the black ghettos. At first, the Panthers tried to persuade the ghetto inhabitants to take matters into their own hands, for example by setting up free breakfast programmes for schoolkids, and by leading campaigns against rent racketeers. But enthusiasm soon faded, and the rhetoric in 'Black Panther' became heavier and heavier. The Panthers soon turned into a nationalist front, flying the flags of Marx, Lenin, Stalin and Kim Il Sung. Placing as much emphasis as they did on leadership, it was their leaders who inevitably came under the fiercest fire when the white reaction came. Many of them ended up in gaol or were neatly shot

DON'T LET THIS HAPPEN...

dead. Steve Gilbert's comic strip 'White Makes Right' tells the tale of one of the party ministers' death.

One result of the Black Power movement was that it inspired a comparable national pride in other ethnic minorities in America, such as Puerto Ricans, Mexicans and Indians. Nor did right-wing groups, such as the extremist American Nazi Party and the Zionists, shun the opportunity to give their image a face lift.

The unpopularity of the war in Vietnam was beginning to show even within the army itself. One of the ways this manifested itself was in GI papers which were circulated illegally in the barracks. The number of such papers grew to several hundred within a few years. We publish here a strip by an artist called Walker from the radical 'Up Against the Wall', which was distributed among American troops stationed in Germany. Earlier, Walker had worked for the underground paper 'Seed'. 'Up Against the Wall' did not find favour among the military authorities, if only because it gave enthusiastic reports of 'fraggings' — the practice of using hand-grenades to blow up superiors who proved too combat-happy. Towards the end of the war mutinies became more and more common. A clever cartoon strip composed of clandestine photographs taken of one such uprising was printed in Chicago's Marxist-Leninist 'Rising Up Angry'.

Elsewhere, too, armies were infiltrated by liberation and protest movements. In the Netherlands in 1970 anonymous cartoons were circulated which incited conscripts to sabotage. As sabotage was already rife in the Dutch army, the military unions as well as the army leadership were far from enchanted. In France and Germany, protest movements shook the armed forces.

A 'Liberation News Service' (LNS) was set up to provide the underground press with news, photo-graphs and graphics. It had its roots in the radical SDS, and though culturally it was in sympathy with the anarchistic spirit of the underground movement, politically it took a stance that owed more to New Left thought. The youth revolution grew up and began to define itself in political terms.

In the strips that appeared in the various magazines, the content came first, technical quality second. The result was that an increasing number of untrained people started to create their own strips to draw attention to their problems. A Boston collective found they could mobilize support with extremely primitively drawn strips. This method of propaganda proved very effective, the awkward drawings illustrating the reality called up by the text. For another example, look at the strip about the International Police Academy. Many of these local strips were reproduced and distributed by the LNS in their weekly information parcels for their members as long as they had a general interest value. You can see the enormous variety existing in the 'movement propaganda' if you look at the childish, direct Boston Collective strip next to the factual and professionally drawn strips about IBM or the Rockefeller family comic book.

The UPS and LNS held a convention for all their members in Washington in 1967, and almost three hundred papers and groups were represented. Allan Katzman of the 'East Village Other' had this to say:

'Today's youth are more concerned with civil rights, the war in Vietnam and poverty. Their involvement is with protecting the freedom of privacy from an encroaching totalitarian technocracy; doing away with barbaric institutions of war; and freeing half the world

Comic from the *Black Panther*, USA, 1971. © *Black Panther*.

(The Black Panther/ LNS)

TO YOU!

from the chains of poverty and starvation.

'Everywhere and especially in America, there is a cultural evolution taking place: an evolution that will sweep Johnson and his ilk, the grey-haired myth of the masters, into the garbage heap of obsolescence. Wisdom and time are now on the side of youth.

'It is the primary purpose of this meeting to pass along this vital information and to convince the young people of America and the world that they are not crazy or alone; that they are wiser than their elders, who persist on a political and economic path which can only lead to total destruction.'

The next day all the representatives at the conference took part in the national march on Washington in protest against the escalation of the Vietnam war. And yet there were enormous contradictions in the group: one sector of the participants at the conference was principally interested in the creation of an alternative way of life; opposing them were those others who, building their protest increasingly on imported ideologies, saw themselves as the intellectual vanguard of the revolution. 'People's Labour', an offshoot of the Maoist 'Second of May Movement', was infiltrating the SDS; the Black Panthers had developed Stalinist leanings, and the Trotskyite Youth Against War and Fascism group tried to gain control over the anti-Vietnam war protest circus. They were less interested in exploitation and oppression on the home front than in world-wide anti-imperialism.

A section of the student movement believed that the workers were still the only class that could create a revolution, and some of them became convinced that the best thing they could do was to stop their studies and work on industrial assembly lines. A section of the students in SDS, however, stayed active in and around the universities, and in the wave of occupations that swept America between 1968 and 1970.

Parallels can be seen in the German student movement, which at the beginning was principally directed at transforming everyday life. And similar vanguard ideas appeared there too as conflict with the authorities escalated and the movement became more politicized. Drop-out students published scores of magazines for industrial workers in which they explained, with the help of simple strip cartoons, just how the workers were being exploited. The workers, however, were as little impressed with alternative lifestyles as they were with the pamphlets of the mainly Marxist-Leninist groups which on their side exhorted them to demand '10 per cent or more' or else go on all-out strike.

The protest movement really regained its momentum only when action started coming from neighbourhoods and grass-roots movements, separate from the students. This form of action was no longer directed at abstractions like 'the consumer society', but rather at more tangible problems, problems of their own living conditions, which people hoped to change for themselves through direct action.

THE PROGRESS OF THE ELDRIDGE (CHESHIRE) CAT

If you're not part of the solution, you're part of the problem.

If you're part of the solution but not the correct part of the solution you're part of the problem.

If you're not part of the correct part of the solution you're a worse part of the problem than the apologists for the problem.

If you're part of the solution who has become part of the problem you've co-opted the solution.

So part of the problem is the solution

If you're part of the solution you're part of the problem.

With apologies to Jules Feiffer.

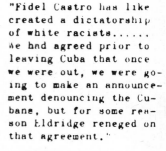

"Fidel Castro has like created a dictatorship of white racists...... We had agreed prior to leaving Cuba that once we were out, we were going to make an announcement denouncing the Cubans, but for some reason Eldridge reneged on that agreement."

Earl Ferrell, former secretary to Eldridge Cleaver

Cover of *Paranoia City*, comic mag. from Switzerland, 1972.

der tödliche Finger

soso, sie sind also ein korrekter Mensch, sie lieben Ruhe, Ordnung & Polizei....

.. arbeiten über 20 Jahre im gleichen Betrieb, beliebt bei Vorgesetzten, keine Vorstrafen; keine Betreibungen....

.... sie jassen, jodeln, lesen die NZZ, glauben an Gott und sind im Schützenverein......

...die Jugend finden sie schlecht, besonders Langhaarige & Dienstverweigerer denn.....

...sie sind Leutnant in der Armee!

höchste Zeit, dass sie verrecken!

Peng!

Comic from *Hotcha*, Switzerland, 1970. © Antonholz Portman.
The Deadly Finger
Well, well, so you are an upright person, you love peace and quiet, law and order... you have worked over twenty years with the same company, your boss likes you, you have never been criticized, never any complaints... you play cards, you read the *Neue Zürcher Zeitung*, believe in God and belong to the shooting club... you're a lieutenant in the army!... about time you were bumped off!

'Love the police', a pamphlet from Switzerland, 1969.
DOGS, WILL YOU BITE FOREVER?
Is the policeman a heartless machine? No, he has feelings. He'd rather have FUN and SEX than a truncheon.
Proposal: golden truncheons as mascots for our friends and allies. Rubber truncheons are softer and less valuable.
The Zurich police are animal-lovers. They allow their dogs to play with demonstrators. Therefore: bones for our fourlegged friends.
Policemen aren't criminals, they are as peace-loving as other citizens. They only make a nuisance of themselves because they are ordered to do so by the government. 'Get lost, cur!'
(For how long will peaceful passers-by and apolitical pop fans continue to be beaten to a pulp? For as long as they remain peaceful.)
Therefore: turn passers-by into demonstrators. Take progressive workers, schoolkids and students.

Willem, strip in *De Witte Krant*, one of the first Dutch underground magazines, Netherlands, 1967.

1. '...and day in, day out, nothing to do but lie here.' 2. 'Then why don't you go and read something?' 3. 'Nothing is as boring as the underground press.'

Königin Julianas Europatraum

Auszüge aus der Rede ihrer kgl. Majestät anlässlich ihres Staatsbesuchs in Frankreich

„Unsere Meinungen können manchmal auseinandergehen über den sichersten und schnellsten Weg....

aber das Ziel, das wir alle anstreben, ist ein wirklich lebendiges und belebtes Europa...

das dank seiner vielfältigen Einheit kühn die dringenden Aufgaben und die noch unerforschten Gebiete, welche uns die menschliche Verantwortung noch offenhält, meistern kann...

Die Dritte Welt, die zwei Drittel der Menschheit umfasst, wird auf unser beständiges Interesse zählen können..."

The dream of Queen Juliana of the Netherlands, Switzerland, 1972.
© Nachrichten für Unzufriedenen.

QUEEN JULIANA'S EUROPEAN DREAM
Extract from Her Royal Highness's speech on the occasion of her state visit to France.

1. We may sometimes disagree as to the safest and quickest road... 2. But the goal we all seek is a living and dynamic Europe... 3. (Factory closed)... that by its unity will be able to find a solution to the serious problems of the underdeveloped regions which weigh heavily on our responsibilities. 4. The Third World, which encompasses two-thirds of the world's population, can count on our continuing interest.

Four pages from a Swedish comic about the Russian Revolution, Sweden, 1968. © *Puss*.

All Power to the soviets! The interim government responds with an order to the troops to shoot the demonstrators. 400 dead.

Pravda is banned.

Lenin hides out in Finland and writes *State and Revolution.* **The proletariat state cannot wait until the bourgeois state has abdicated: a violent revolution will be necessary.**

2. During Lenin's absence, the Bolsheviks gather for their Seventh Congress. Dark clouds of unrest build up. The new false god of the bourgeoisie, general Kornilow, tries to become a dictator. Through the resoluteness of the people, the counterrevolution is foiled.

3. After Kornilow's failed coup, nothing can keep the people from joining the revolutionary movement en mass. Workers, farmers and soldiers take up the cry of the Bolsheviks: Power to the soviets! —Trotsky, the great agitator — Stalin, the fanatical revolutionary.

'Stand up, the world's rejects!...'

The liberals accuse them of excessive revolutionary fervour. But an omelet can't be cooked without breaking the eggs.

The next time October!

4. Disguised as an engine driver on a steam locomotive, Lenin returns to Petrograd from exile in Finland. When everyone is present, Lenin arrives. He is clean-shaven and wears a wig as a disguise. The central committee decides to speak out in favour of armed rebellion.

la grève

FOURBERIE

DESESPOIR

PRISE DE CONSCIENCE

Andy Capp gets wise, Belgium, 1969. © *Liaisons.*
THE STRIKE
Betrayal
1. 'Hey, here's the shop steward.' 2. 'Good news! we won!' 3. 'Did we get what we wanted?' 'No, not exactly, but the boss did give in!' 4. 'Congratulations.' 'He gave me a cigar.'
Despair
5. 'Well, at least the union got something out of it!'
A new consciousness
6. 'You know, the shop steward has just decided to call another strike!' 'He's too fond of cigars...you'll see!' 9. 'At the next strike, that's the first thing we'll do.'

Right: Change leaders, not your life. Belgium, 1972. © *Noir.*
Mobilization
1. After decades of genocide in Vietnam...'We must do something'. 'Hear, hear.' 2. So they organize a demonstration against US imperialism. 'Peace in Vietnam!' 'US go home.' 3. Thousands of corpses in Biafra... 'Gentlemen, if we accept this, we accept anything.' 'He's right.' 4. And a demonstration once again gathers together all those who have a heart: 'Stop the war!' 5. In Palestine there are also problems...'They are a tragic people.' 'Let's help them.' 'It's our duty.' 6. 'Long live free Palestine.' 7. 'Suppose we now talk about our own problems?' 'Egoist! Enemy of the People! Those bourgeois intellectuals ought to be shot!'

93

94

JOSKE

Cover of a comic book about the dole, Belgium, 1975. © Karlos.

Facing page: Marxist rhetoric combined with Superman images, Sweden, 1968. © *Puss.*

1. A single spark can start a forest fire! 'I must solve this mystery, whatever the price!' 2. 'Workers of the world unite! Ho! Ho! Ho! Take that!' 'Aaargh!!' 3. 'Excuse me!' 4. 'I'll help you if he's that dangerous!' 5 'Long live the Revolution!' 'Right on!' 'The people are nothing without a people's army.' 6. 'Workers of all lands, tonight!' 'We shall overcome!' 7. (Polling station) 'Everything's gonna be OK.' 8. 'Nourish proletarian ideology and destroy bourgeois ideas. Smash the old order.' 9. 'Long live cultural revolution!' 10. Shortly afterwards…'Revolution — never.' 11. Superficially the reactionaries are terrifying, but in reality they are not so strong. 12. The Yankee imperialists and all kinds of dangerous animals have dug their own graves — the funeral isn't far off. 13. The first heir, his son or grandson, has never had to soil his hands with work of any kind. 'Be on your guard.' 14. 'Long live Marxism. Long live the people.' 'To dare to think, to dare to talk openly, to act, to break out.' 15. To plan a break-out, to fail, to try again, to fail again…until they are defeated.

Campaigning against pollution, Belgium, 1970. © *Liaisons.*
1. 'Hello, sir. Are you a soap-powder manufacturer?' 'Yes, sir. The biggest.' 2. 'Sir. Your soap, after washing, leaves 50 per cent of undecomposable waste. Henceforth, to limit pollution, only 20 per cent waste will be allowed. That is the law.' 3. Act passed in 1964. Official publication. 5. Five years pass... 6. 1969. 'Well! Haven't you done anything about it?' 7. 'My dear sir. If an act is to be enforced, it must have an enforcement decree. That's what I'm waiting for.' 8. One year later... 9. 1970. 'Here's the decree!' 10. 'Do they want my blood? Let me at least have the time to find a new formula. Washing powders are chemicals, and chemistry is a slow process. How can you expect overnight changes?...'

'The decree grants you a year's respite.' 11. 'Ah, well!' 12. A year later... 13. 1971. 'Sir, here is the new 'bio-degradable' washing powder. Obviously, it'll cost more.' 14. 1964 to 1971: seven years. Annual production of detergents: 700,000 tons. 50 per cent polluting waste instead of 20 per cent = 30 per cent too much. So, in seven years — and only in France — 1,470,000 tons of excess pollution in the water table, in rivers and oceans. 15. Why seven years? Why 50 per cent? Why 20 per cent? Why not 0 per cent? And how are we going to get rid of those millions of tons? 16. 'I can answer that one for you. We are going to look for a solution. But again it will mean chemical research. And that will take a long time and it will be very expensive. Please help us. Thank you!' Anti-pollution campaign.

HELD OVER BY FASCIST DEMAND!

SO UNSETTLING, SO GRIMLY MELODRAMATIC THAT YOU WON'T SOON FORGET IT...

THE CAPITALIST POWER STRUCTURE PRESENTS:

PIG JUSTICE

AN IN-DEPTH LOOK AT FASCISM IN MODERN-DAY BABYLON

WITH AN ALL-STAR CAST OF BLACK PANTHERS

HUEY NEWTON, BOBBY SEALE, DAVID HILLIARD, ELDRIDGE CLEAVER, CHARLES BURSEY, THE NEW YORK 21, THE CONNECTICUT 8, AND MANY, MANY MORE.....

AND A SUPPORTING CAST OF THOUSANDS OF PIGS, PUPPETS, PAWNS AND PROFITEERS, ALL OUT FOR BLOOD!!

YOU ASKED FOR IT, MR. AND MRS. AMERICA...

HEAR THE TRUMPED-UP CHARGES...SEE THE JURIES OF NON-PEERS...SEE THE FASCIST JUDGES AND THEIR RUNNING DOG PROSECUTORS RAILROAD THE VANGUARD REVOLUTIONARIES

NOW PLAYING AT KANGAROO COURTS NATIONWIDE

EXECUTIVE PRODUCER: TRICKYDICK NIXON
DIRECTED BY: J. EDGAR HOG

P RATED FOR POLITICALLY MATURE AUDIENCES ONLY.

WARNING: THIS MAMMOTH PRODUCTION IS EXCEEDINGLY COSTLY, AND PIGS BEING PIGS, THEY ARE NOT WILLING TO PUT UP THE ENTIRE COST OF THEIR OWN PRODUCTION, AND THEREFOR ARE SUBJECTING THE BLACK PANTHER PARTY TO ARMED ROBBERY IN THE FORM OF EXORBITANT BAIL (RANSOM), AND FINES (EXTORTION). THE PARTY NEEDS YOUR FINANCIAL SUPPORT. SEND ALL CONTRIBUTIONS TO: BLACK PANTHER PARTY NATL. HQ.— 3106 SHATTUCK AVE.— BERKELEY, CA 94705

Playing at Kangaroo courts nationwide in the USA, 1970. © *Black Panther*.

TO BE CONTINUED?

The deportation of 'Big Man' from Germany, USA, 1967. © *Black Panther*.

ATROCITY COMICS PRESENTS: **WHITE MAKES RIGHT!** THE STORY OF LAW AND ORDER IN THE GHETTO

STEVE GILBERT

The murder of Fred Hampton, USA, 1970.

A comic book explaining what a Spick is, USA, 1970.

A comic by and for Navaho Indians, USA, 1971. © Dine Baa Hani.

Who is supporting whom?

A comic from the Chicano trade union, USA, 1969. © El Malcriado.

Strip of the American Nazi Party, USA, 1967.

The "mentality" of today!!

Do you recommend the use of NARCOTICS? — NO

Do you believe in the practices of ABORTION, PORNOGRAPHY and HOMOSEXUALITY? — NO

Are you longing for the blessings of the SOVIET-DEMOCRACY? — NO

Are you in favour of STREET TERRORISM and BLACKMAIL by the press? — NO

Do you approve of the EXTERMINATION of the WHITE RACE? — NO

you bloody, dirty FASCIST MONSTER!!

dec. 1967

Dutch Fascist comic strip, reprinted in England, 1967. © *Europa Post.*

The promised land, USA, 1972. © *Israel & Palestine.*

a tale of the Baal Shem Tov
by *Kirschen.*

A DEAF MAN PASSED A WEDDING FEAST AND SAW THE GUESTS DANCING...

THE MUSICIANS TOO, LEAPED AND SPUN TO THE STRAINS OF THE SONGS...

AND HE SAW THE LOOKS OF ECSTASY ON THEIR FACES, AND HE SAW THEM SPIN AND LEAP, BUT BECAUSE HE WAS DEAF HE DIDN'T HEAR THE MUSIC... AND HE BELIEVED THEM ALL MAD... AND HE LEFT.

AND SO IT IS THAT MANY OF OUR BROTHERS AND SISTERS ARE UNABLE TO HEAR THE MUSIC THAT TOUCHES OUR SOULS. BUT THE DAY WILL COME WHEN THEY TOO WILL HEAR THE SONG OF LIBERATION...THE SONG OF ZION... AND THEY TOO WILL JOIN OUR DANCE... *AM YISROEL CHAI !*

Comic from the *Jewish Liberation Journal*, USA, 1970.
© **Jewish Liberation Project.**

Facing page: Anti-Communist comic for all the family, USA, 1968.

WHY WE CAN'T LET IT HAPPEN HERE !!!

TO BE CONTINUED......

When Company A Said "No!"

From BOND

Comic from the *Bond*, one of the first GI magazines, USA, 1973.

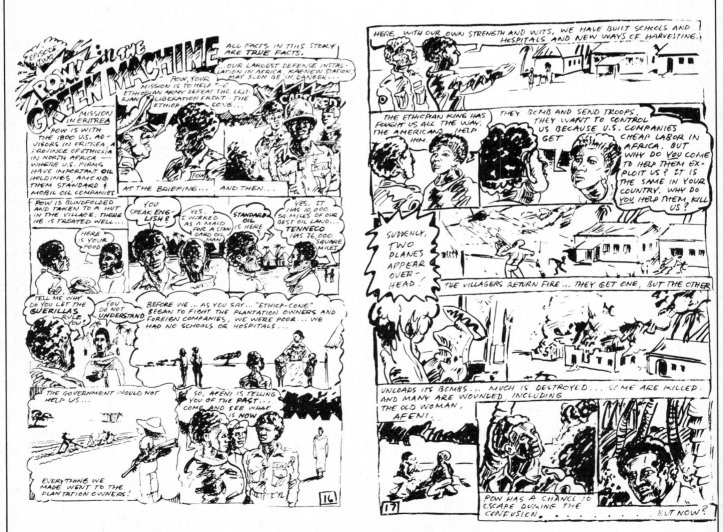

Two pages from *Up Against the Wall*, an illegal magazine for American GIs in Berlin, USA, 1970.

HOW TO GET IN OUT OF THE DRAFT

BY WALTER

TOO FAT — TOO THIN

MUSCULO-SKELETAL DEFECTS

SEVERE INGROWN TOENAIL

GENITAL-URINARY DEFECTS

MISSING TRIGGER FINGERS

OBSCENE TATTOOS

PSYCHIATRIC DISORDERS

TOO TALL — TOO SHORT

ACNE and/or FLAT FEET

PUNCTURED EARDRUMS

EYE DEFECTS

STIFFENING OF JOINTS

Anti-military service strip, USA, 1968. © *The Seed*.

The GIs draw up the petition eventually signed by sixty-six men that resulted in total American withdrawal from the base.

The grunts ignore Cronin as he enters machine gun bunker five.

Captain Cronin (left), the Commanding Officer at Pace, and an unidentified major interrogate Chris (center), first of the six grunts to refuse to go on patrol.

In the 1969 battle of Queson, Alpha Company refused to go on fighting in one of a long list of rebellions by GIs in Vietnam.

Secretly photographed mutiny in Vietnam, later printed as a strip, USA, 1971. © *Rising Up Angry.*

Strip poster distributed by the radical French magazine *Soldats en Lutte,* **France, 1970.** © **Les Temps Modernes.**

I am a creep	A blackleg, a telltale	I bluster I boast	I am going to get my head kicked in

S no. 1

De militaire dienst is in de eerste plaats een hersenspoeling om de soldaten aan te passen aan de regels van deze maatschappij en zodoende de bestaande uitbuiting voort te zetten en de rust en orde te handhaven.
De verplichte Geestelijke Verzorging vormt daarvan eveneens een onderdeel. Hoewel b.v. de 'kritiese' aalmoezenier Keesen toegeeft;" inderdaad, de dienst kan als het ware als een hersenspoeling werken, waardoor allerlei zaken, die dat vroeger niet waren, ineens zeer vanzelfsprekend worden ", (Volkskrant 10 dec. '69) maakt hij daar zelf ook deel van uit.
Het gaat niet om een vraagstuk van oorlog en vrede of geweld en geweldloosheid, maar om een klassetegenstelling tussen de bazen en hun arbeiders en tussen de officieren en hun soldaten.

Erger dan de Geestelijke Verzorging zijn de bij het leger aangesloten psychologen, psychiaters, sociologen en ander afgestudeerd tuig, dat er op uit is om met jullie te doen wat zij willen.
Ex-legerpsychiater in een interview met Vrij Nederland (6 dec. '69):
" De dienstplicht is ongelooflijk belangrijk voor de doorsnee Hollandse jongen, zowel uit lichamelijk als uit geestelijk (!) oogpunt.... mijn zoons hebben (in dienst) een hoop geleerd: leiding geven, in een groep opgaan, niet je eigen zin volgen maar je naar discipline schikken. Waar leer je dat anders?.... Als je een leger hebt moet je dat gebruiken (!) om de dienstplichtigen demokratie-minded te maken ".

LAAT JE NIET LANGER BELAZEREN !!

Sabotage pamphlet, Netherlands, 1970.
For Soldiers. Appears irregularly. Free
1. The captain thinks this is the right moment... 'Sergeant, get those chaps into line.' 'Yessir.' 2. ...to give a peptalk put together by the army psychologists. 'From a bunch of civvie nincompoops we have made you into...' 3. and tries to persuade them that they need discipline. '...men, chaps who know what they want: AUTHORITY!' 4. National Service is tough, but it makes chaps healthy.
National Serivce is first and foremost a system of brainwashing to adapt soldiers to the rules of society and thus to perpetuate exploitation by maintaining law and order. The compulsory Mental Health programme is part of this. Although the 'critical' chaplain, Keesen, was quoted in the *Volkskrant* as saying that military service can work as a form of brainwashing, where all kinds of things become acceptable where they may not have been before, he himself is part of that system.
The issue is not one of war and peace, or strength and weakness, but it is a class struggle between bosses and workers and between officers and soldiers.
Worse than the Mental Health programme is the army's army of psychologists, psychiatrists, sociologists and other graduate parasites, who aim to do what they like with you.
Ex-army psychiatrist in an interview in *Vrij Nederland* (6 December 1969): 'The National Service is incredibly important for the average Dutch youth, physically as well as spiritually (!)...my sons have learnt a lot (in the service): leadership, group spirit, self-discipline. Where else would they learn that? If you have an army, you should make use of it (!) to make the serviceman democratic-minded.'
DON'T LET YOURSELF BE CONNED!
TAKE THE LEADERSHIP INTO YOUR OWN HANDS!

DE DIENST VREET AAN JE KLOTEN

NA TWEE WEKEN JEZELF AFRUKKEN WEET JE NAUWELIJKS NOG WAT HET IS OM EEN VROUW TE NEUKEN

Terwijl een impotente sergeant zich al schreeuwend staat op te geilen, worden soldaten zoet gehouden met uitputtende eksersities en kamfer in het eten.
Je mag maar één keer in de twee weken weg, en krijgt dan een treinkaartje naar het adres van je ouders. Als je vriendinnetje in een andere plaats woont moet je daar op eigen kosten heen. Aan soldaten die volgens de burgelijke moraal getrouwd zijn, wordt wel toegestaan om s'avonds bij hun vrouw te slapen.
Als je niet getrouwd bent moet je je geil maar twee weken ophouden, of je kwakkie in je baret lozen.
Maar zelfs het afrukken wordt op alle mogelijke manieren tegengegaan, door krakende bedden en open w.c.'s. Nergens kun je een rustig plekje vinden om je eens lekker af te trekken.

ER ZIJN NOG ANDERE MANIEREN OM JE TE BEVREDIGEN !

+ saboteer uit seksuele behoefte
+ saboteer uit wraak
+ saboteer voor je plezier
+ saboteer uit sensatie
+ saboteer om je te drukken
+ saboteer uit ellende
+ saboteer om er beter van te worden
+ saboteer uit verveling
+ saboteer om politieke redenen
+ saboteer voor je eigen best-wil
+ saboteer voor je vrijheid

S no. 2

POSTBUS 2179 AMSTERDAM

Illegal sabotage pamphlet, Netherlands, 1970.
NATIONAL SERVICE CHEWS UP YOUR BALLS
After two weeks of jerking yourself off, you hardly know what it is any more...to screw a woman.
While an impotent sergeant works himself up by yelling, soldiers are kept quiet with exhausting exercises and bromide in their tea. You are only allowed out once a fortnight, and you get a train ticket to your **parents' home town.** If your girlfriend happens to live in another town, you have to get there at your own expense. As for soldiers who have married in obedience to the bourgeois ethic, they are allowed to sleep with their wives at night. If you are not married you just have to hold back for two weeks, or else relieve yourself into your beret.
But even masturbation is made as difficult as possible, with **creaking bunks** and open toilets. A nice quiet place for wanking is impossible to find.
There are still other ways to get satisfaction!
1. The terror of training... 'Idiot!' 2. is revenged in the evening. 'Take that, sergeant.' 3. The sergeant is never to get up again...
sabotage for sexual desire
sabotage for revenge
sabotage for pleasure
sabotage for sensation
sabotage for self-expression
sabotage out of misery
sabotage to improve yourself
sabotage out of boredom
sabotage for political reasons
sabotage for your own good
sabotage for freedom

Illegal sabotage pamphlet, Netherlands, 1970.

Comic about the International Police Academy, USA, 1970. © CRV.

We talk a lot about what we don't want: Wars, hate, boring jobs, boring schools, degrading welfare, stockings that run as soon as you put them on, high rents for junky apartments, poisons in our food, water + air, getting hassled and attacked on the streets...

WHAT DO YOU WOMEN WANT, ANYWAY??

WELL... to think about the good times in the bad times takes a lot of thinking. Because we don't just want Equal Pay for Equally Bad Jobs or lady generals in Imperialist Wars. We do want women to have control over their own lives, free child care, the right to have children when they want to. And we want to make sure that all those services — health care, housing, food, clothing, transportation, and education should be controlled by the **PEOPLE** and **FREE**. We don't want to just patch up a sinking ship. We want to launch a new one.

In September we met in Philadelphia for the Plenary Session of the People's Constitutional Convention called by the Black Panther Party, and women from different backgrounds had lots of trouble talking to each other. To get to know each other better and to begin to make plans for the kind of world we want, we're having a conference for Women from the Boston AREA, Saturday, **NOVEMBER 14**, at 232 Bay State Rd, Boston (Boston UNIVERSITY WOMEN'S CENTER) from 11AM to 5PM. There will be Day Care, so bring the kids and bring something for lunch. For more information call 492-4130.

Pamphlet of Boston Propaganda Collective, USA, 1970.

HERE IT IS FOLKS! THE **NEW** SUPER DELUXE AMERICAN IMPERIAL!

NOW BEFORE I MENTION THE PRICE, LET ME TELL YOU WHAT WENT INTO THE **MAKING** OF THIS AUTOMOBILE.

ALUMINUM FOR THE ENGINE AND TRANSMISSION FROM SURINAM, HAITI, AND JAMAICA.
CHROME FOR ALLOYS AND TRIM FROM TURKEY, SOUTH AFRICA AND PHILIPPINES.
TUNGSTEN FOR ALLOYS FROM BOLIVIA, THAILAND, SOUTH KOREA, AND BURMA.
TIN FOR ALLOYS FROM INDONESIA, MALAYA, BOLIVIA AND CONGO.
COPPER FOR THE ELECTRICAL SYSTEM FROM RHODESIA, CANADA AND CONGO.
RUBBER FOR TIRES FROM MALAYA AND INDONESIA.
OIL FOR LUBRICATION AND FUEL FROM VENEZUELA AND THE MID EAST.
AND LOTS MORE!

WE USED TO RIP-OFF LOTS OF COPPER FROM CHILE BEFORE THEY NATIONALIZED IT. LATER FOR **THEM**.

IT TAKES AMERIKAN INGENUITY AND KNOW-HOW TO ORGANIZE THIS GLOBAL RIP-OFF AND TURN IT INTO A FINE LOOKING AUTOMOBILE. SO WHEN YOU HEAR THE MELLOW SOUND OF YOUR NEW AMERICAN IMPERIAL V-8, YOU CAN FEEL A WARM SENSE OF PRIDE IN KNOWING **WHY** YOUR SON DIED IN VIETNAM.

The American 'Imperial', from *Fixing Brakes, A People's Repair Manual*, USA, 1972. © People's Press.

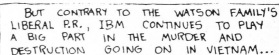

From a series of comics exposing big multi-national companies, USA, 1972. © *Pittsburg Fair Witness.*

Exposing the machinery of the system, USA, 1969. © *Leviathan.*

Cover of a comic book about the Rockefeller family, USA, 1973. © Joel Andreas.

Those Fabulous Furry Freak brothers fight infiltration, USA, 1969. © Gilbert Shelton.

Alternative lifestyles develop, USA, 1971. © *Hundred Flowers.*

Six different Mao comics, USA, *c.* 1970-72. © *Le-Ru, Quicksilver Times, Berkeley Tribe, The Free You.*

PIECE NOW?

LE-RU-'70

WE DO NOT WANT WAR.

WE ARE ADVOCATES OF THE ABOLITION OF WAR.

BUT WAR CAN ONLY BE ABOLISHED THROUGH WAR.

AND IN ORDER TO GET RID OF THE GUN, IT IS NECESSARY TO TAKE UP THE GUN.

WHAT MUST WE DO TO WIN?

EVERYTHING REACTIONARY IS THE SAME.

IF YOU DON'T HIT IT, IT WON'T FALL.

IT'S LIKE SWEEPING THE FLOOR...

WHERE THE BROOM DOESN'T REACH, THE DUST WILL NOT VANISH.

THE ENEMY WILL NOT PERISH OF HIMSELF.

★ ★ ★ ★ ★

WHAT IS A REVOLUTION?

LE RU 70

IS THE REVOLUTION A DINNER PARTY?

NOPE!

IS IT WRITING AN ESSAY?

NOPE!

IS IT PAINTING A PICTURE?

(NOPE!)

IS IT DOING DOPE?

NOPE!

A REVOLUTION IS CLASS STRUGGLE LEADING TO A FINAL VICTORY FOR THE PEOPLE!

★ ★ ★ ★ ★

THE WORLD IS AT A TURNING POINT

THERE'S A SAYING THAT EITHER THE EAST WIND IS STRONGER THAN THE WEST WIND — OR THE WEST WIND IS STRONGER THAN THE EAST WIND.

TODAY THE EAST WIND IS STRONGER THAN WEST WIND.

THAT IS TO SAY THE FORCES OF SOCIALISM ARE STRONGER THAN THE FORCES OF IMPERIALISM.

Damn students, damn workers, Canada, 1969. © Georgia Straight.

Facing page: 'The eagle may have great wings, but…', USA, 1972. © Berkeley Tribe.

Why they call it 'take-home pay', USA, 1972. © *Rising Up Angry.*

Classes in Revolution, USA, 1970. © *Good Times.*

What's left of the 'New Left', USA, 1979. © Jay Kinney.

s.d.s. ~ The Amerikan Komiks!

My folks busted their humps to send me to college

But I tc k up with SDS, the Third World and Revolution. I dug the grass bit and balling them radical chicks

I blew my mind on Mao, Che and Marcuse. Man, it was revolution all over the scene. We even burned the library, not to mention flags and draft cards

It wasn't all easy, though. I got the clap from the chicks..and last Fall I called a TPF pig & motherfucker and he broke my front teeth. My folks sent bread for new choppers

In May, I hit a capitalist with a bottle and the bastard broke my nose. Our chief acid head, Mark Rudd, told us to snuggle up to our black brothers so

I went to a Panther rally and they broke my new teeth and the other arm. I got 30 days for being a bum. Well, SDS is dead now. The Panthers hate our guts and the Army won't have me. I wonder if the folks still live in the same old place?

A well-developed consciousness, USA, 1969. © *Other Scenes.*

From the toilet roll of history, USA, 1970. © *Good Times.*

WE DEMAND:

1 That the United States government end its systematic oppression of political dissidents and release all political prisoners such as Bobby Seale and other members of the Black Panther Party.

2 That the United States government cease its escalation of the Vietnam War into Cambodia and Laos; that it unilaterally and immediately withdraw all forces from Southeast Asia.

3 That the universities end their complicity with the United States war machine by the immediate end to defense research, ROTC, counterinsurgency research, and all other such programs.

STRIKE!

Student strike poster, USA, 1970.

121

After the North Vietnamese film *People's War* was forbidden in Edison High School a riot broke out and Philadelphia chief of police Rizzo sent in 300 cops. USA, 1970. © *Philadelphia Free Press*.

Facing page: The March on Washington, USA, 1969. © *East Village Other*.

EINEN FINGER KANN MAN BRECHEN, FÜNF FINGER SIND EINE FAUST

Five fingers make a fist, Germany, 1971. © *Revolutionärer Kampf.* One finger can be broken, five fingers make a fist.

Comic from a revolutionary paper distributed amongst workers at the BMW factory, Germany, 1971. Let's turn the wage rounds into a fight round!

Another from the same magazine, Germany, 1971.
1. A student is distributing pamphlets. White-collar worker: 'Why don't you try working first?' 2. Graduate who tried working first. 'You'll have to do more work before you can make any demands.' 'Yessir, Mr Director.'

German treatment of Italian left-wing comic character Casparazzo, Germany, 1973. © *Wir Wollen Alles.*
1. (Bread and wine shop). 'One pound and one litre.' 2. 'Yes, yes! the currency crisis.' 3. 'Half a pound and three-quarters of a litre.' 4. 'Devalue, revalue, float?' 5 'A quarter of a pound and half a litre.' 6 'Wage freeze! ...then prices will be stabilized.' 7. 'One glass of wine and a slice of bread.' 8. 'Luckily, the economic situation is improving!' 9. (Guns).

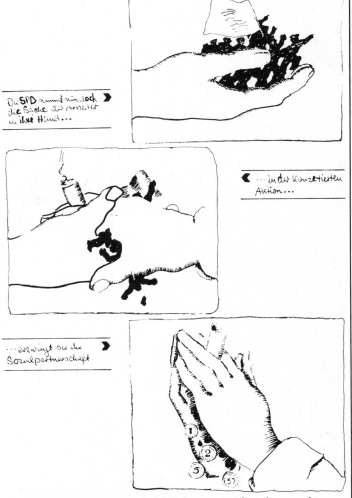

Artists co-operate with young factory workers to expose bad working conditions, Germany, 1970. © Arbeitskreis Progressive Kunst.
About good bosses and angry apprentices — POLITICAL STRIPS
Anyone can make political strips. Write and draw about what's wrong in your factory or college. That way your comrades in other places will get to know about it. We want to publish this kind of comic strip and distribute it. Write to:...

Marxist criticism of how the Social Democrats conduct the annual wage-negotiations, Germany, 1970. © *Arbeiterkampf.*
1. The SPD has finally taken up the workers' cause... 2. ...with concentrated action... 3. ...it presses for social harmony.

Cover of anti-authoritarian comic book for kids, Germany, 1972.
© Dr Tesi Faushieder.
2...4...6...8...is this where greedy-guts meets his fate? An exciting story of Indians, vagabonds, capitalists, and there is always a woman in it, etc. For all Mickey Mouse fans, all kids and Marx and Engels readers. 'I don't get anything to eat.' 'Help, help, help, help.' — and many tips.

Facing page:
Comic about the mythological alliance of workers and students, Germany (Berlin), 1970. © *883*.

DECISION IN BERLIN

1. This is Berlin by night! More precisely, Kreuzberg. All is peaceful — or is it? 2. What's this? It looks as if a number of houses stand empty in the middle of the city! 3. Some houses are only partially empty. A few floors are occupied by 'guest' workers. 4. But we're not very hospitable to our 'guests'...some have to pay 150 marks for a bed! Students also live in these houses. They're not much better off... 5. How is this possible in a city where so many houses are empty? 6. Who can solve this riddle? Perhaps Mr Mosch? Or Wiese & Co? They own 525 houses in Berlin alone.
'These houses are worth at least 950 million marks!' 7. 'But why then are you leaving them empty?' 'Well..it is the fashion these days for large companies to build their offices in the Kreuzberg district. They'll pay anything, and the longer I wait, the more I earn!' 8. 'But I thought that you don't have permission to demolish many of those houses!' 'Well, so I let those for the time being to students and Italians. If I don't repair them, they'll soon be ripe for demolition.' 9. 'Then, I sell them and earn a few million! ...and then I'm really set up! Ha, ha.' 10. Meanwhile, in another part of town! A worker, his wife and seven children have been living here for five years... 11. ...in a two-room flat. The welfare system couldn't find them a house...Suddenly, the bell rings and a young man appears at the door... 'Are you ready?' 'Of course!' 12. And then they remove all the furniture in those two rooms... 13. ...load it into a waiting van which drives off at great speed... 14. ...through the slumbering city, en route to its destination! 15. Meanwhile, in one of those vacant houses, lots of things are going on... 16. Workers and students are renovating the house. The students learn how tough life is (as if they didn't know about it already!). 17. But most of them are experienced at wiring, papering, etc. The children especially enjoy themselves hugely. 18. Another few hours' work, and everyone has a roof above his head. They move in the furniture, they make it cosy, and then everybody goes to bed! 19. The next day a press release is issued: '...also prepared to pay a reasonable rent...' 20. And now the fun starts: on one side, the landlords, on the other, the tenants. 'Citizens of Berlin, whose side are you on?' 'Mr Policeman, how much rent do you pay?' 'Don't just stand there with your mouth open, why don't you do something to help?'

126

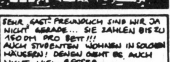

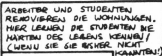

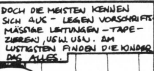

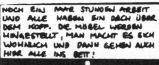

Comic exposing Fascist mantle organization (Aktion Widerstand), Germany, 1972. © *Arbeiterkampf*.
1. 'Ladies and gentlemen, as you know we always strive to give you the news truthfully.' 2. 'Ten minutes ago, we announced to you the discovery of a terrorist arms arsenal.' 3. 'With regret we must retract this announcement.' 4. 'The parties involved have just informed us that it wasn't a terrorist arsenal after all, but the equipment of a local rifle club. Our apologies.'

Facing page:
Four pages of a comic book for young workers, Germany, 1973. © Basis Verlag.
APPRENTICE FRONT
1. First day at work: he reported to the boss and got an earful of words, words... 'We're very happy to have you! Nice workmates! You'll feel at home here. If there is anything troubling you, just come and see me. Your wages will be excellent!' 2. 'Can you come up for a minute to show round our new apprentice?' 3. 'This is your instructor, Mr Hahn. Please show our young friend around.' 4. 'The last one is the apprentice locker.' 5. 'But it's already full!' 'You can still squeeze your coat in there.' 6. 'Idiot!' 7. 'The place is fully air-conditioned.' 'To give you a chance to have a good look round...' (Finally, a new sweeper!)' 8. '...why don't you start with some sweeping.' 'Bloody hell, you'd better first discuss with the boss whether I'm supposed to be a mechanic or a charwoman.' 9. 'Take the broom!' 10. 'Watch out! They'll make a housewife of you yet!' 11. 'Stop chattering! Sweep!' 12. 'Hey, you idiot!' 'Am I doing something wrong?'

Old Bavarian folk hero brought up to date by Guido Zingerl, Germany, 1971. © *Berliner Extra.*

1. BAVARIAN HIASL. 2. First: Bavarian Hiasl lectures his comrades on the particulars of the Bavarian class struggle. 3. Bavarian Hiasl drives out the devil and frees the lakes. (The beach is for everybody.) 4. Bavarian Hiasl wards off the rent vampire with the sign of the cross. 5. Bavarian Hiasl expels the gnomes from the Ministry of Education. (Education for everybody. Gnome school. Good, but stupid.)

Comic from 'Red Help' (organization for gaoled left-wing activists), Germany, 1971. © Rote Hilfe.

1. 'Hey, Mickey, that copper wants to arrest us!' 'Oh Goofy, it must be a misunderstanding. After all, we are innocent citizens!' 2. (Court house) 'Hurry up, the judge doesn't have all day.' 3. 'Your Honour, what's the meaning of this? We're surely not common criminals?' 'I'll decide about that for myself, thank you!' 4. 'Lock them up in Cell 13!' 'But...Your Honour...' 5. 'Listen, there must be some mistake!' 'That's what they all say!' 6. 'In with you!'

Capitalism hurts men and women, but women more, Germany, 1970.
CAPITALISM ATTACKS BOTH MEN AND WOMEN…
3: …BUT THE WOMEN MORE! Kurt Knap's wages: 155 marks. Ursula Knap's wages: 99 marks. 5. Community creche. 7. …AND THEREFORE ALSO CHILDREN!

1. AND IT SABOTAGES LOVE! 2. I just can't go on like this. Other women are just as badly off! Something must be done! 3. No automatization and sackings; but automatization and training! Solidarity creates strength, only strong individuals can change this! 1 Starfighter = 6 creches, 95 crashed Starfighters = 570 creches! We want to create our own working conditions! Don't begrudge it, lower the rents! Our weakness is our strength! Creche-leaders: we are on strike! Women should no longer remain accomplices! After fifty years of emancipation, our pay is still terrible! 4. That was the foreman. 'We won't allow them to control us any more, we are going to get ourselves organized! For a community where we can have children without going under! Where technical progress won't be used against us! Where men, women and children can be people.'

The revolt of the comic characters, Germany, 1971.
ANNI & BELLO
Once upon a time there was an editorial meeting at Ana & Bela. 1. '...and we must continue to fight against the profiteers, with renewed energy, and we want, and we can, and we shall...' 'Dopey, the people must be kept totally informed.' 'Rubbish, we should do something completely different.' 'Perhaps a song: The East is red, tralalala, or...?' 'Perhaps a comic strip?' 2. 'That's it! A comic strip about Anni and Bello, the fearless. They will contribute in word and deed to education of the proletarian masses impoverished by consumer-oriented rubbish.' 'Great idea!' 3. 'Gosh, what bores! Come on, Bello, we're getting out of here.' 4. 'Hey, what's this? You can't just leave. We need you for a comic strip.' 'You must be mad, we're not going to let you fill our text bubbles with your idiotic slogans!' 'Show some solidarity.' 5. Where on earth did you get that idea?! You are an idea that belongs to us, and you do what we want, you hear?' 'Ungrateful creatures!' 6. 'Have you got parsley in your ears? How do you like this argument? Pretty sound, huh?' 'Great.' 7. 'That bloody frame!' 'For the last time, we won't allow you to put words into our mouths!' 'Yes, but...' 8. 'Yes, but...' 'What an idea! Everyone to fill in his own balloon...' 'We'll go and find some other friends.' 'Great.'

134

Strip about expropriation, Germany (Berlin),
c. 1972.
2. Private ownership. Dispossession is fun!
3. Capitalist: 'Ha, ha…leisure makes them
prepared to go back to work. Vulgar yobs!' 'How
long are we going to sit back and take their bloody
capitalist relationship?' 4. 'Young workers,
students, schoolkids! Come on! Let's go and
inspect that private property from close up!'
5. 'If you want things to change… You must do
something to change them!' 6-7. Attack the
capitalist where he's not expecting it! 8. Let's
build barricades for the future with the past!
9. Occupations are reported from every section
of the city. 10. Develop a revolutionary
imagination! 11. 'Handle property questions
with flexibility!'

PEOPLE'S PARK

At the beginning of 1968 the University of Berkeley acquired about thirty houses, which were to be pulled down as part of their expansion projects. Around one hundred students were living in these houses. Their cries of protest were lost in the general noise of scores of other protests staged at the university at that time, and the houses were torn down at the end of the summer. Construction of the new buildings might take anything up to ten years, and in the meantime the space was to function as a parking lot. The next year, on 20 May, a few of the people living nearby spontaneously took the initiative of planting some greenery on the empty lot. As the work progressed, the number of enthusiasts grew. Young and old all mucked in to turn the lot into a park. A kind of community sprang up around the projected park, and in the weekends hundreds of people turned up at the site. Nobody was eager for a confrontation with the authorities; nevertheless, the authorities felt they couldn't just allow this situation to continue. The university's administrators were afraid to lose control over the space, and announced that a fence would be erected around their property. After a week of doublefaced dealings with a working group from the neighbourhood, the university announced that a fence would definitely be erected. Ironically, that very day saw the appearance of a report by the town council entitled 'Land, Beauty, Food and Mutual Respect', with the subtitle 'Gardens of Harmony'. The report suggested that people without gardens be encouraged to ask large landowners for small pieces of terrain on loan. According to the report, the owners would undoubtedly react positively if the petitioners showed respect for 'life, freedom and another's property'. Whether inspired by the elegant phrases of the report or not, at a large meeting, the residents decided not to give up 'People's Park' without a struggle. The following morning at half past four 250 policemen stormed the park and threw out the hundred-odd occupants who had spent the night there. All the streets around the park were closed off and policemen armed with rifles were posted on the roof-tops, while workers began erecting a fence. A few hours later the news had spread and thousands of people came streaming to the site. A doomed attempt to reoccupy the park turned into a pitched street battle between protesters and police, with the police using small shot and tear gas on the rioters. The battle lasted all day, fed by police reinforcements that were rushed in from neighbouring districts. The next day a curfew was imposed and Governor Reagan sent in a contingent of 2,000 National Guardsmen. But even that didn't stem the tide of demonstrations and street battles. A demonstrator wounded on the first day, James Rector, died in hospital. The National Guardsmen began to lose confidence in the justice of their cause, and at one point even countermanded orders by refusing to don their gas masks. The gassing of the crowds went ahead anyway, but by helicopter, which sprayed the crowds below. A lot of people were badly burned. As the fighting wore on, it was decided to stake out a new park somewhere else. The new site chosen was significant: it was a vacant lot created by the Bay Area Rapid Transport (BART) project. BART had been devised to link the city's business centre with the wealthy suburbs. No provision had been made for a station in the black neighbourhood through which it sliced its way, Hunter's Point. Predictably, the police made short work of the new park scheme.

The struggle for People's Park is typical of the spontaneous resistance shown when new-found creativity drives people to stop being passive in the face of the tyranny of society's status quo. The status quo, on the other hand, sees this new resistance as a deadly threat, and, once it has succeeded in controlling it by police methods, it attempts to defuse it at other levels to 'bring it into line'. What happened in Berkeley, and what earlier happened in Harlem and Watts, served as the basis for the tasks of the Urban Coalition, set up in 1967. The Urban Coalition examined the backgrounds to such outbursts in order to prevent repeat performances. Progressives, conservatives, trade-unionists, mayors and all kinds of other groups formed the Coalition. With the help of government and Ford Foundation subsidies and full support from the nation's academia, they were ready to put the cities back on their feet. Big projects were created to provide employment and so make the ghettoes thrive. For that was the whole objective: to cool down the seething ghettoes. And so it was only appropriate that 'Business Week' should call the noble urban planners the 'anti-rioters'.

Adventures in real estate, USA, 1971.

TENANTS RISING

published with the help of the BERKELEY TRIBE and the Black Panther Party
AN OFFICIAL PUBLICATION OF THE BERKELEY TENANT'S UNION. and it's **Free!** **N⁰8**
and featuring **TENANT TOONS** by Amerika's best known criminologist. Chester Ghouled

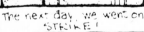

Cover of the Berkeley Tenants' Union paper, USA, 1970.

PARIS MAY '68

In 1968 student unrest reached its climax. In America, the occupation of Columbia led to violence between students and police. The occupation was characterized by the solidarity as well as the tension between the SDS and the Black Students' Afro-American Society, who had adapted Black Power slogans to their own needs — a demand for 'black culture' to be taught at the university. Another aspect of the Columbia revolt was the close co-operation between the students and the local residents, whose homes were threatened by the university's expansion programme.

But unrest was not confined to America. In France, students at Nanterre had been campaigning since the beginning of the year against regulations forbidding male students from visiting girls' rooms. The university authorities were not prepared to meet the students' demands and called in the police to break up the demonstrators. A group of students calling themselves the 'enragés' had contacts with the IS, and influenced the others into shifting the emphasis of their protest from the minor issue of visiting rules to the educational system itself. On 22 March the arrest of six students led to a brief occupation of the university administration buildings, which ended when the six students were released. But fearing more demonstrations, the university's chancellor Grappin ordered the university to be shut down and called in over five hundred police to seal off the campus. The demands for a democratization of the system grew more radical, and students started to boycott exams. On 2 April the central auditorium was occupied by some 1500 students. Speakers included representatives of the German SDS, and the possibility of setting up a 'critical' university was examined.

Group discussions, work committees, posters and pamphlets mushroomed while the authorities hoped that the Easter break would bring peace. Meanwhile Fascist strong-arm squads threatened to teach the students a lesson and, though nothing actually happened, it became clear that violence would soon erupt. Fearing this, Grappin closed the university again, and in protest the students called a meeting at the Sorbonne in Paris. Some of the members of the 'Mouvement du 22 Mars' (M22M) disrupted a few lectures there to draw attention to the protest meeting. Rector Jean Roche smelled trouble and warned the French riot police. At half past five the Sorbonne was cleared of the demonstrators and five hundred students were arrested. The presence for weeks of police on the Nanterre campus had made hardly any impression, but at the Sorbonne it was another matter. Demonstrations were held the whole of that weekend, and there were some fierce clashes with the police. Many more students were arrested. The more established student groups were taken totally by

138

"REASON ASSAULTS THE VIEWER, IMPRESSION ENVELOPS AND SEDUCES HIM TV ONLY USES REASON TO SUPPORT PREJUDICE"

surprise by the events and hardly knew which side to take. The Trotskyite Fédération des Etudiants Révolutionnaires (FER) and the Union Nationale des Etudiants (UNEF) expressed their solidarity from the beginning, but the Communist press and student union dissociated themselves from disturbances which they claimed prevented the children of the working class from studying and thus sabotaged their true struggle for democracy. The idea of the M22M on the other hand was that this student rebellion was not just aimed at improvements in the universities, but that it put into question the whole social structure responsible for making the universities function as they did:

'Why are the students angry?

'The papers write about idiots, about a "golden" youth that wants to hide its emptiness by means of violence and vandalism.

'What purpose lies behind such articles?

'Just one: to isolate the students from the workers, to caricature their struggle and misrepresent it in order to make them shut up.

'Three thousand students fought the cops last Friday — are they the "handful of vandals" Minister of State Peyrefitte talked about? NO.

'We fight because we refuse to become:

'—professors or teachers at the mercy of the select-tion process on which the educational system is based, to the detriment of the children of the working class;

'— sociologists whose job it is to think up campaign slogans for the government;

'— psychologists who see to it that the motivations that inspire the "working units" are in harmony with the interests of the big bosses;

'— academics whose research is of interest only to the profit-oriented economy.

'We don't want a future as "watchdogs". We don't want courses that prepare us for such a future. We don't want exams and degrees as reward for accepting the system and agreeing to work within its limits. We refuse to back up the bourgeois university. We want to change her radically, so that university-trained intellectuals may march alongside the workers. Wherever you are, come and fight bourgeois oppression!'

The M22M concentrated more and more on the workers' cause. Already at the first sit-in at Nanterre it had been proposed that the university's doors should be thrown open to all the workers in the district.

As the conflict spread throughout France, its aims became more universal. On 6 May, the breaking-up of a demonstration led to fierce street fighting, and the first barricades were erected in the Quartier Latin. The next day an overwhelming majority of the students voted for a strike. Faculty members and university employees joined in. The ensuing demonstration totalled 50,000 marchers. The students' demands were amnesty for those arrested and a complete withdrawal of police guards from the Sorbonne. At this stage the trade unions were spurred on by their younger members to join in, and in Lyon a youthful branch of the CFDT (Confédération Francaise Démocratique du Travail) marched side by side with the students. The lycée students then came out on strike in large numbers. The Communists, meanwhile, did their utmost to stem the tide of protests with lies and clichés — thereby succeeding in putting themselves out of the picture.

The crunch came on Saturday, 10 May; with the outbreak of the fiercest battles in Paris so far. The traditional student quarter was totally sealed off by over sixty barricades. Police charges were repelled with paving stones, molotov cocktails and home-made smoke bombs. Hundreds were injured. Nor was it just students who were involved, as was evident from the masses of household goods flung into the streets below by local residents. In view of these developments the trade unions — the CFDT and the Communist CGT (Confédération Générale du Travail) called a general strike for Monday, 13 May. Protest against police action was coupled with wage claims and demands for better pensions. The demonstration on the 13th was unprecedently broad-based. Estimates put the number of marchers at anywhere between half a million and one million. Meanwhile Prime Minister Pompidou had given in to the demand that the Sorbonne be cleared of police, and promised to consider the question of amnesty for the arrested students. The university was immediately taken over by the students again and turned into a discussion forum for all the people of Paris. The doors were open to everyone. Street gangs, action groups of all kinds, artists, teachers, delegations of young workers from various industries were all welcomed. On the night of 14 May word was out that workers at the Sud-Aviation Company had occupied their factory and were holding the chairman hostage. When two days later the Renault workers occupied their plant, there was no stopping the tide. Student-worker co-operation became closer, and a wave of sit-ins swept the whole country. On 24 May de Gaulle announced that there would be a referendum, and while fighting continued in the streets the trade unions began negotiations with the government.

Charles Seguy, Secretary General of the Communist Party (PCF), called the outcome of the talks a victory; but the workers — for example those at the Renault plant — saw things differently — not a single political demand was granted. Nothing about self-rule, not a word about a people's government. Seguy had made his feelings about self-government clear on 22 May, in the paper 'L'Humanité': 'The movement that is in the hands of the workers is much too powerful to let itself be stopped by hollow phrases like "self-government".' It became obvious, perhaps for the first time, to many of those involved in the protest movement that the trade unions were hardly a positive, supporting force as far as fundamental social changes went, and that they had but one objective: to strengthen their own position of power within the existing system. A demonstration against the agreement between the government and union leaders was labelled 'provocation' in the Communist press. And when the country's traditional opposition —

parties and unions — stepped up the propaganda for a massive 'no' vote in de Gaulle's referendum, the power question was relegated for all practical purposes to the poll-box. Then on 31 May de Gaulle announced on television that the referendum would be postponed and there would be a general election. Meanwhile he had had secret consultations with army leaders, who had assured him of their support. For the time being, however, de Gaulle called in the other troops at his command: the Gaullist Action Civique, which took hundreds of thousands of its petit-bourgeois supporters, frightened by recent events, into the streets. The tide had turned. The unions joined in and appointed new shop stewards for all branches of industry. Riot police moved in to occupy the Renault plant at Flins. And even though new strikes continued to erupt, and the barricades reappeared at one point in Paris, it became clear that the movement was on its last legs by the middle of June.

The May revolution gave rise to an unusual outburst of creativity, not least in the field of comic strips. Largely responsible for this was the Conseil pour le Maintien des Occupations (Council for the Maintenance of Occupations), a group of forty to fifty Situationists and 'enragés' who had broken away from the M22M. On 17 May the group participated in the sit-in at the National Institute of Pedagogy. With the co-operation of a printing works (IPN) which had also been occupied, masses of propaganda was churned out in the form of posters, pamphlets, stories in strip-form, etc. Print runs reached up to a quarter of a million. Some of the leaflets appeared in several languages, and at least forty comics were published. Very soon strips originating from the occupied factories started appearing — from Sud-Aviation for example. But the spray can was still by far the most effective and popular method of propaganda, and slogans and drawings appeared on walls everywhere.

May 1968 made a huge impact on French political life, and in its wake appeared a great number of new publications which tried to avoid dogmatic analysis. Two of these were 'La Cause du Peuple' and 'Action', which first appeared during the May uprising. Some strips that appeared in these papers are reproduced here. Two of the best French political cartoonists, Siné and Wolinski, were 'Action' contributors; Siné later left to work on a new paper, 'L'Enragé'. This paper also recruited the Dutch artist Willem.

'Idiot International', a paper published both in London and in Paris, made a deliberate effort to start a discussion between the different political splinter-groups. The comic strips in this paper poked fun indiscriminately at the gauchiste establishment and at the jargon of the revolutionaries.

Later the growth of the underground in France saw the appearance of new comic papers like 'Zinc' and 'Anatheme'. But their success was shortlived, unlike the more satirically oriented 'Hara Kiri', 'Le Canard Enchainé', 'Charlie Hebdo' and 'La Gueulle Ouverte'.

Comic strips were so popular that they also appeared as street posters. In Toulouse a comic-strip poster newspaper appeared on walls for several years; it was called the 'Contre-Journal'.

Le Progrès Social!

« Que vous soyez payé à la pièce ou au temps, quand êtes-vous payé ? En d'autres termes, pendant combien de temps faites-vous crédit à votre patron avant de recevoir le prix du travail effectué ? Etes-vous payé à la semaine, au mois... ? »

Marx, L'enquête ouvrière.

Social progress, *Cahiers du Mai*, France, 1970.
© *Cahiers du Mai.*

Social Progress!
1. Grandad: 'In the old days we were paid weekly.' Dad: 'With me, it was monthly.' Son: 'When I started it was bi-annually, but now they pay me at the end of the year.' Grandson: 'Well, as for me, my boss says I'll get paid every forty-five years.' 2. Grandson's wedding day. 'OK, I haven't got much, but I get paid every half-century!' 3. Later... 'Only twenty-seven more years to wait...perhaps they'll give me an advance.' 4. Years later... 'Is that the bell? Open the door, sonny.' 'Yes, dad.' 5. 'What is it?' 6. They unwrap it... 7. Surprise? 8. 'Ah! Your toys have arrived!'
'Whether it's at a piece rate or at an hourly rate, when are you actually paid? In other words, how long do you give your boss free credit before receiving payment for work you have done? Are you paid weekly, or monthly...?' — Marx.

REVOLUTION MAN

Revolution Man in *Idiot International*, England, 1970. © *Idiot International*.

One of the first comics of the CMDO, France, 1968.
1. '*Les enragés* do publish exceedingly funny comics.'
'Curiously, all they do is change the bubbles.'
'Isn't this a manifestation of a new concept of revolutionary practice?'

2. 'Of course! The subversion of the comic strip, the graphic form of proletarian expression, means the bypassing of bourgeois art.' 3. Seconds later... 'Ah...don't shoot!' 'SI! (Situationist International)' 'Well, no... poor idiots...we're just too lazy to draw our own pictures.'

LA DERATISATION

Poujade ministre de l'environnement

First page of a continuing comic about the 'gauchist milieu', in *Idiot International*, a paper published in France and England aiming to regroup different left-wing tendencies, France, 1970. © *Idiot International*.

Rat Extermination

1. One evening, in a normal middle-class house, in a normal middle-class neighbourhood... 2. Normal?? 'You take an empty bottle...first put in some soap and sand, then you half-fill it with petrol...half-full only, mind, not to the top...well then you stop the neck with a greasy cloth...' 3. 'Light it, and throw it...' Bang! 4. 'Throw it, throw it, yeah, that's all very well, but you need to know *where* to throw it...' 5. 'That's easy, just switch on the radio...' 6. '...the unprecedented events in Nanterre...' 'Aargh Marcellin!' 'It can't go on like this! We must do something!'

Poujade, Minister of the Environment, France, 1970.
© *Idiot International*.
1. 'Three months' suspended sentence for having impersonated a bird to attract the authorities' attention.' 2. 'Even victims of industrial accidents could help in the improvement of the environment.' 3. 'We must solve problems where we find them...blah, blah.' 'Well shit then, let's go!' 4. 'There are'nt any maids' rooms in council flats.' 5. 'We'll take care of your environment, little fellows!!' 'Something's always happening, tralala, at the Galeries Lafayette.' 6. 'I shall not walk on the grass again.' 7. 'Who said that the middle class is an enormous ass and the people an enormous foot? Who said that?' 'I dare you to say that again!' 8. 'Pah! That has nothing to do with the environment.' 9. 'In the end we'll find a philosophy yet for this goddam whore, the Fifth Republic!'

Wolinski in *Action*, a paper published by the student committees, France, 1968.
1. 'Finally finally the young are waking up.' 'Bravo bravo.' 2. 'Finally they show us the way.' 'Bravo, little ones.' 3. 'Young man, the future is yours.' 'It's yours.' 4. 'But don't you dare touch the present! and leave the past alone!'

Propaganda from the campaign 'No holidays for the rich', France, 1970.
1. 'And what did you do this year?' 2. 'Oh, this and that, we punched up the bosses and the cops that we were pissed off with... We fought the so-called 'independent' unions, UNIC, for example...' 3. 'And also the union heavies...at Renault-Billancourt, for example.' 4. 'We locked up some bosses here and there — at Usinor-Dunkerque and elsewhere...' 5. 'As for sabotage, I can't say that we've been idle — you remember Dunkerque? Well there've been hundreds of others all over the country. Disruptions, revenge on the bosses' crimes — they call them "work accidents".' 6. 'At Vallourec, we tried a bit of everything but when it came to getting rid of the cops, it was a real united front...' 'And this summer? Are you taking a rest? Are you going on holiday?' 'Don't be daft! You sound like a horoscope in *France-Dimanche*! Oh, it's really going to get hot this summer, don't you think?'

Facing page: First page of a comic about the occupation of the Lip Factory, France, 1973. © La Cause du Peuple.
1. LIP STORY   First stage: Authority challenged. The multinational trust ASUAG gets a stake in the Lip company through its Swiss subsidiary Ébauche S.A. 17 April 1973: The crisis breaks. The managing director, Mr Saintesprit, is sacked by the bankers. Two administrators are appointed. Ébauche S.A. wants to scrap everything except the assembly line. 2. 12 June 1973: The administrators meet the shop stewards. The Lip workers, assembled on the lawn, hear over loudspeakers that their wages have been docked as of 10 June. They storm the offices and hold the administrators hostage. In their briefcases are found detailed plans for mass redundancies. At 23.45 the Chief of Police sends in the troops. The administrators are released...and the cops are hailed with stones. 3. THE GREATEST HOLD-UP OF THE CENTURY That evening, a group of brave lads of the Action Committee and the CFDT choose a new hostage: the stocks of watches. Dédé, little Louis, Gessie and Pierrot bring cars. While Rizi and fat Georges busily empty the fridges (the watches are kept cool for preservation), Lola stuffs them into the baskets and Momo heaves them into the cars. 4. Second stage: 'It is possible: we can manufacture, we can sell, we can pay our own wages.' 18 June 1973: The shop stewards and the Action Committee put a motion to the assembled workers: to manufacture watches and to sell them themselves. After half-an-hour's reflection time, the motion is accepted unanimously. 5. Sales committee: The watches are sold at a 42 per cent discount. Client-friends eagerly stream in... Administration committee: Accounts are public. Sales figures are shown on noticeboards. When they have taken over the factory, the Lip workers find thousands of watches in odd corners — evidence of the criminal negligence, anarchy and pillage of the former bosses.

HISTOIRE DE LIP

1° PERIODE: L'AUTORITÉ CONTESTÉE

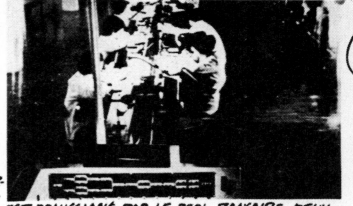

LE TRUST MULTINATIONAL ASUAG A PRIS UNE PAR-TICIPATION DANS L'ENTREPRISE LIP PAR L'INTER-MEDIAIRE DE SA FILIALE SUISSE ÉBAUCHE S.A.

17 AVRIL 73: LA CRISE ÉCLATE: LE P.D.G. MONSIEUR SAINTESPRIT EST DEMISSIONÉ PAR LE POOL BANCAIRE. DEUX ADMINISTRATEURS SONT NOMMÉS. EBAUCHE S.A. NE VEUT CONSERVER QUE LA CHAINE DE MONTAGE-

12 JUIN 73: LES ADMINISTRATEURS RENCONTRENT LES DÉLÉ-GUÉS. LES LIP REUNIS SUR LA PELOUSE APPRENNENT PAR HAUT-PARLEUR QU'ILS NE SONT PLUS PAYES DE-PUIS LE 10 JUIN, ILS SE PRECIPITENT DANS LE BU-REAU ET LES SEQUES-TRENT. DANS LEURS SER-VIETTES SONT DECOUVERTS DES PLANS DE LICENCI-EMENTS PRECIS. 23H45 LE PRÉFET ENVOIE SES GARDES MOBILES. LES ADMINISTRATEURS SONT RELACHÉS... ET LES FLICS RECONDUITS A COUP DE PIERRES...

LE PLUS GRAND HOLD-UP DU SIECLE

Le même soir, un groupe de gars courageux... du Comité d'Action et de la CFDT choisissent un nouvel otage: les stocks de montres. Dédé, Petit louis, Gennie et Pierrot amènent les voitures. Les montres étaient au frais (pour la con-servation) tandis que Rizi et le gros Georges s'escrimaient à vider les frigos, Lola bourrait des paniers et Momo les trim-ballait jusqu'aux bagnoles en cavalant à travers la paierie.

2° PERIODE:

"C'EST POSSI-BLE, ON FABRI-QUE, ON VEND, ON SE PAYE"

18 JUIN 73: LES DÉ-LÉGUÉS ET LE COMITÉ D'ACTION PROPOSENT A TOUT LE PERSONNEL, EN ASSEM-BLÉE GÉNÉRALE DE FABRI-QUER DES MONTRES ET DE LES VENDRE. APRÈS UNE DEMI-HEURE DE PAUSE POUR RÉFLÉCHIR, LE PROJET EST ADOPTÉ A L'UNANIMITÉ

COMMISSION VENTE: LES MONTRES SONT VENDUES AVEC 42% DE RÉDUCTION. LES CLIENTS-AMIS AFFLUENT...

COMISSION GESTION → LES COMPTES SONT PUBLICS. PRODUIT DE LA VENTE, DE LA SOLI-DARITÉ SONT AF-FICHES. EN PRE-NANT LE CONTRO-LE DE L'USINE, LES LIP ONT DÉ-COUVERT DES MILLIERS DE MON-TRES DANS TOUS LES COINS. GASPILLAGE, ANARCHIE ET PILLAGE PATRONAUX

Vente de montres

Recettes	Total à ce jour
	23/7 6.10.460'

Today's literature is tomorrow's ad copy, England, 1971. © *Mole Express.*

A comic discussing the methods of the group that published it, France, 1970. © *Cahiers de Mai.*

1. 'But where are they going?!...The workers aren't ready yet for the social revolution.' 2. 'Power to the workers.' 3. Does the failure of a programme mean that its objectives are utopian, illusory? When extreme leftist groups seeking a social revolution find out that, since May '68, their efforts to infiltrate the working class have been in vain, does this mean the working class has become bourgeois and resists any revolutionary ideas? Or do they simply only resent one particular programme? There is no doubt in the minds of the militants grouped around the *Cahiers*. It is the programme that should be reviewed.

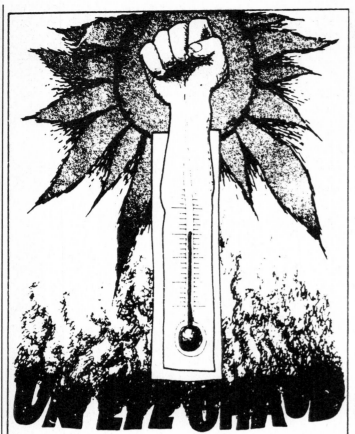

The promise of a 'hot summer', France, 1970. A HOT SUMMER — Magazine of the 27 May Movement
1. A hot summer. 2. No holidays for the rich. 3. Holidays for the workers. Private property. Keep out.

First page of a comic by and for secondary school kids
(*Les Lycéens*), France, 1972.
Nixon — murderer
Immediate withdrawal of the GIs
Stop the bombing!
1. In the very heart of the USA, the anti-war movement. 'But?!?*! Isn't it illegal? 2. 'Come on everybody, to the demo!' 3. 'You do support us, don't you? Will you come to the demonstration, huh?' 'What...whatever you want, Mr Dalton!' 4. A little later... 'The demonstration has passed a resolution...' 5. 'Immediate withdrawal of the troops? Are you guys mad? You bunch of drug addicts! nihilists! delinquents!' 6. 'Is even Lucky Luke joining in? I think I'm going crazy!'

About sexual misery, France, 1973. © *École du Mai.*
1. 'The more I make love the more I feel like making revolution; the more I make revolution the more I feel like making love.' ' "You shouldn't mix up fun...and class warfare." (J. Duclos).' 2. 'Why can't we make love?' 3. Because we grow up in the midst of sadness and conjugal strife, the holy family with its hypocrisy and taboos. 4. Because, in the social hell of adolescence, we jerk off secretly behind the cellar door, or on the back seat of a car: they have even made masturbation a guilt-laden crime. 'That's him! He's guilty! He's responsible for everything!' 5. Because the girl is scared, because the guy is embarrassed, because there's nowhere to do it...because it has to be done quickly and furtively. 6. Because we're brainwashed, castrated by those impotent, frigid, vegetating mummies, teachers, lecturers, etc... 'Stop it!' 7. Because in order to get on the Pill, you have to be twenty-one years old, or suck up to a cop-doctor or a cop-chemist. 8. Because having destroyed all human relationships, the consumer society offers us as substitute for sex: 'Birkin's ass.' 'B.B's tits.' 'The thighs of the panty-hose ads.' A world of hallucinations, where subjectivity is locked away, where all desire is abandoned in favour of the dominant images of consumerism. 9. Because in boys' schools the exaggeration of the myth of virility, teasing and boasting don't soothe, but rather strengthen the boy's real frustration. 10. Because in girls' schools girls are indoctrinated with the image of the Couple, the social pattern of sexual misery, and are encouraged to sacrifice the fun of today for the married bliss of tomorrow.

Right: Comic reporting an effort to evict a family in Roubaix, France, 1972. © *Pour la Justice.*
1. That morning, Maître Perrard, bailiff, launched his troops into battle with his fearful war-cry: 'MONEY!!' 2. Eager to ransom the poor, he was after the few sparse sticks of furniture possessed by the Duhayon family. 3. The father: 'We'd rather smash up the furniture we've still got...' 4. The son: '...rather than give it up to Perrard.' 5. Meanwhile, upstairs, the mother: 'If we had any money we'd gladly give it to see you go. Piss off with your coppers and leave us alone!'

Anti-racist strip from small satirical magazine, *La Côte d'Alerte*, Dijon, a region where many immigrant workers live, France, 1973.
© *La Côte d'Alerte.*
1. 'Get to work! (Ah! just like the good old days!)'   2. 'Sir, we are happy to offer you the job of foreman, in consideration of your experience…'
3. '…and your understanding of — umm — Arabs —am I right?'   4. 'I should say so! I know those lazy bastards.'   5. 'Sign here — by the way, do you know Arabic?'   6. 'No, why? … They're here now so they can bloody well speak French like the rest of us!'

What to do after school, a comic satirizing efforts of the police to attract youngsters, France, 1972. © *Technique en Lutte.*
1. Vacancies.   2. 'No vacancies!'   3. 'I do have a job going, for 3 francs 10 per hour.'   4. 'No vacancies.'   5. 'Nothing! Nothing! It's the same story everywhere! I can't stay at home without a job! Or with a pittance of a wage! What the hell am I going to do?'   6. Join the police. A man's career.   7. Barracks. Police station. Join up!
When the bosses have no use for us, they'd like to see us join the ranks of their khaki-clad slaves!

CONFERENCE SUR LES OPERATIONS
ELEMENTAIRES DE MAINTIEN DE L'ORDRE
ET EXERCICES PRATIQUES
PAR LES

UNITES D'INSTRUCTION
du FORT de CHARENTON

From a police manual, instructions in riot control, France, 1970.
Lessons in the elementary tactics of law enforcement and practical exercises.
By the training corps of the Fort of Charenton.

Right: Comic strip from Toulouse, France, 1971. © Mlle Taillefer

STRIKE
Fun! fun! fun!
From Batignolles to Faulquemont via the ORTF, Biarritz-Shoes, the ports of Marseille and Brest, the air traffic controllers, the demonstrators of the vineyard workers…and everything else that they're keeping secret from us!
TREMBLE, BOURGEOIS
Your welfare society, your new society
EVERYTHING'S BREAKING UP!
The workers need nobody to organize themselves
Sangui the Toulouse Strangler
1. *La Dépêche:* The Toulouse Strangler finds new victims. 2. Mrs Supercop Baylet, publisher of *La Dépêche*, leads the investigation herself. 'There aren't enough policemen, I have to interfere…I bet it's an Arab.' 3. Nobody feels safe any more in this city — the fear of being strangled at any moment… 'I understand how you feel, but it mustn't discourage us from fighting for better days.' 4. 'We'll stop all those stranglers one day.' 5. 'What? The Toulouse Strangler has been unmasked! By the people! Sanguinetti! It's Sanguinetti and his gang…' 6. 'Yes, come quickly, to 44 Rue Bayard in front of his offices.' 7. At 44 Rue Bayard, while the cops look the other way and Mrs Baylet pretends to see nothing, the Toulouse Strangler is pushed out of the window. The crowd gets ready to lynch his accomplices, who had been strangling the freedom of Sud-Aviation, Onio, Pac, on the street and everywhere. 8. Bosses should be locked up… and headmasters too! Read *Crève Salope* (Die, Bastard). To be continued…

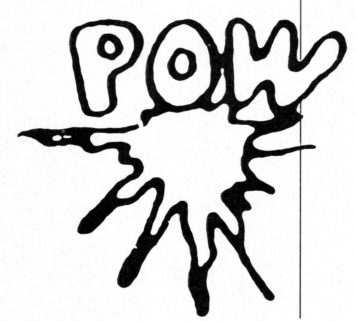

Facing page: Tarzan, cop of the jungle, France, 1972. © Gertrude.
TARZAN or the misery of heroism
1. My creator dreamt of making me the lord of the jungle. 2. But I think I have become the lord of shits. 3. Do you realize, under the pretence of tame equatorial capers… 4. …I've shown off to the whole world! 5. While I haven't actually replaced the police. 'Die, dog.' 6. I have played their game by stalking adventurers pointed out to me as being particularly asocial and dangerous… 'Bang!' 'Hey! I think he's around here somewhere.' 7. I have become the accomplice of all sorts of political regimes… 'Is that him? D'you think he'd like to?' 'Of course.' 8. Thinking vainly that I was liberating several primitive tribes from the yoke of their small oppressors, or from the threats of their witch doctors, 9. I only helped to speed up the process of their integration into capitalist or bureaucratic societies where new tyrants and priests were to find a second youth… 10. 'Tarzan! Tarzan! I want you! I need you! But — what are you doing?' 'I have repulsed the advances of the most beautiful women who throw themselves at me, when I would have done better to… 11. …take them instead of satisfying myself with the embraces of panthers and the caresses of she-monkeys.' 'Oooh! wouldn't he be handsome without his loincloth!' 12. 'You've seen it for yourselves, Tarzan's in a fix!' 'Is it bad?' 'I don't know! Will he be able to get out of it?' 13. Well? will he be able to get out of it? Has Tarzan not become too lucid and too talkative? 14. To find the answer, read on…
The story so far: Tarzan talks too much and thinks too much. What's going to happen to him?
1. And so, bit by bit, I became a masochist. I invented tortures for my personal use. 2. My gestures and habits became effeminate. 'Ah! I feel so languid!' 3. I addressed my prayers to I know not what mysterious god: 'You are the east!' 'You are the west!' 4. Finally I became syndicated! 'Join the United Features Syndicate!' 5. Thus I had become a perfect militant… 'Attack when you hear my war-cry!' 6. Millions of readers, locked in a horrible nightmare, will soon identify with my sad self. 7. 'Hey boys! what's the matter with our friend? He's crazy, no? Yeah!' 'Ah! What can I do? I believe there is only one solution:' 8. DEATH or… 9. The revolutionary fight which alone can make me master of my own fate. 10. So Tarzan went to join his comrades-in-arms incognito… 11. And thus begins the first real adventure of TARZAN.

Tarzan

OU MISERE DE L'HEROISME

L'AUTEUR DE MES JOURS RÊVAIT DE FAIRE DE MOI LE SEIGNEUR DE LA JUNGLE

MAIS JE CROIS QUE JE SUIS TRES VITE DEVENU LE ROI DES CONS...

RENDEZ VOUS COMPTE : SOUS LE PRETEXTE D'INSIPIDES GAMBADES EQUATORIALES ET AUTRES ESCALADES

...JE ME SUIS MONTRE EN SPECTACLE DANS LE MONDE ENTIER!

AAAAAAAAHHHH!

QUAND JE NE ME SUIS PAS SUBSTITUE A ELLES...

MEURS DONC, CHIEN!

J'AI FAIT LE JEU DE TOUTES LES POLICES EN TRAQUANT QUELQUES AVENTURISTES QUE L'ON ME DESIGNAIT COMME ETRES PARTICULIEREMENT ASOCIAUX ET NEFASTES..

HEY! ON DIRAIT QU'IL EST PAR ICI!

PAW

JE ME SUIS FAIT LE COMPLICE DE TOUS LES REGIMES POLITIQUES...

C'EST LUI? TU CROIS QU'IL VOUDRA BIEN?

MAIS OUI!

CROYANT LIBERER QUELQUES PEUPLADES

PRIMITIVES DU JOUG DE PETITS TYRANS QUI LES OPPRIMAIT OU DES MENACES DE SORCIERS SAUVAGES QUI LES EFFRAYAIENT

JE N'AI FAIT QUE FACILITER LE PROCESSUS DE LEUR INTEGRATION A LA SOCIETE CAPITALISTE OU BUREAUCRATIQUE DANS LESQUELLES TYRANNEAUX ET NOUVEAUX PRETRES ALLAIENT RETROUVER UNE SECONDE JEUNESSE!...

J'AI REPOUSSE LES PLUS BELLES FEMMES QUI S'OFFRAIENT A MOI ET QUE J'AURAIS MIEUX FAIT DE...

TARZAN! TARZAN! J'AI ENVIE DE TOI! MAIS? QUE FAIS TU?

PRENDRE SUR LE CHAMP AU LIEU DE ME CONTENTER DE L'ETREINTE DES PANTHERES ET DES CARESSES DES GUENONS

AH! QU'IL SERAIT BEAU SANS SON PAGNE DE CUIR!

VOUS AVEZ VU...TARZAN EST EN CRISE!

...JE NE SAIS PAS! POURRA-T-IL MEME S'EN SORTIR?

C'EST GRAVE?

OUI! POURRA-T-IL S'EN SORTIR? TARZAN N'EST-IL PAS DEVENU TROP LUCIDE ET TROP LOQUACE AUSSI??...

VOUS L'APPRENDREZ BIENTOT SI VOUS LISEZ ENCORE **Tarzan**

Tarzan

RESUME DU CHAPITRE PRECEDENT : TARZAN PARLE TROP ET PENSE PLUS ENCORE QUEL VA ETRE SON SORT?

AINSI, PEU A PEU, JE SUIS DEVENU MASOCHISTE. J'AI INVENTE QUELQUES TORTURES A USAGE PERSONNEL

MES GESTES ET MES MANIERES SE SONT TRES VITE FEMINISES

AH!.. QUELLE LANGUEUR!

MES PRIERES SE SONT ADRESSEES VERS JE NE SAIS QUEL DIEU OBSCUR!

ITE MISA EST! ITE MISA OUEST!

ENFIN JE ME SUIS SYNDIQUE!

ADHEREZ AU UNITED FEATURES SYNDICATE ⊕

© AUTHENTIQUE

AINSI J'ETAIS DEVENU UN MILITANT PARFAIT...

QUAND VOUS ENTENDREZ MON CRI DE GUERRE VOUS VOUS ELANCEREZ!

DES MILLIONS DE LECTEURS, CONFINES DANS CET ATROCE RÊVE CLOS, S'IDENTIFIANT BIENTOT A MA TRISTE PERSONNE.

HEY BOYS! WHAT'S THE MATTER WITH OUR FRIEND! HE'S CRAZY, NO? YEAH!

AH! COMMENT S'EN SORTIR? JE CROIS QU' IL NE NOUS RESTE PLUS QUE CETTE ALTERNATIVE:

LA MORT

OU...

LA LUTTE REVOLUTIONNAIRE QUI SEULE ME RENDRA MAITRE DE MA VIE!

POM

PUIS TARZAN S'EN FUT, ANONYME, REJOINDRE SES CAMARADES EN LUTTE...

AINSI COMMENCA LA PREMIERE ET VERITABLE AVENTURE DE LA VIE DE

Tarzan

Council Communist comic, France, 1972.
© Gertrude.

1. A spirit has haunted the world since the nineteenth century… 'Uh! Heavens!'   2. But the decades have rolled by…Revolutions have failed… Material goods and … 'Oh! Great! The man himself.'   3. …the ideological recuperation of Stalinism or Maoism contributed to the confusion… 'I even castrated them to make them more productive…'   4. which reached even us here in the form of those surrogate lefties … May/June 1968…'Ah! at last we'll be able to liberate our repressed desires!'   5. May/June 1970… 'Shit! It's those little leftist jerks again, and their premature ejaculations…'

6. Other derivative revolutionary spirits were quickly invented but were soon revealed to be nothing but horrible little mystical gnomes… 'Hurray for happenings!' 'Up Cybernetics!'   7. …while the spectacular monster still deals in goods composed of human bits and pieces from bodies that are still warm… 'Our ''dormitory city'' will be really revolutionary…' '…yes, down to its recreational facilities…'   8. Nevertheless all the ruling classes, from the bureaucrats of Moscow and Peking to the millionaires of Washington and Tokyo, feel dangerously threatened. They are haunted by a new spectre, more shocking, more terrible, but beautiful, radical, alive with the most wishful expectations: WORKERS' COUNCILS!

Serve...the people. France, 1972. © Vroutsch.
VAMP STORY
1. At the People's Blood-pub
Any breakages will be per-suck-uted
To the slaughter, comrades!
Good drink, drink blood
The blood bank gives credit

Services of the blood-sucker not included
To drink, blood, to drink, blood
(*Drinks:* **Blood — cold Blood — hot Blood — tea Blood — berry Blood — thirsty Blood money — Blood alcohol**)
2. 'And for me a large tray please with a little warm water in it, honourable blood brother.'   'A little surprise, a present for me...'
3. Hehehe, get your hands off — it's mine!   I'm not sharing it with anyone!

THE SPECTRE OF THE OCCUPATIONS

A wave of occupations swept the world as far as Mexico, Czechoslovakia and Yugoslavia. In 1968 local communities seized upon the new weapon, and organized squatters started to take over houses in Holland, Denmark and England. In Copenhagen, a group of squatters aided by neighbours put up a considerable fight when police tried to evict them. In Amsterdam, a group calling itself Buro de Kraker (Squatters' Bureau) began its first campaign in Amsterdam's Dapperbuurt neighbourhood, while in London the London Squatters Campaign was settling in nicely.

The squatters' actions could not do much to solve the housing shortage, most acutely felt by the young, who are generally overlooked when it comes to allotting homes. What they did do was to expose the whole housing system, with its rules and regulations, as a bureaucratic con trick to camouflage the disgraceful housing situation.

After a couple of try-outs that served to draw attention to the plight of the homeless in London, a number of families were moved into some houses in Redbridge that had stood empty for years. The move was backed by local residents, who were opposed to the Council's redevelopment plans. More houses were occupied, then given a facelift. Redbridge Council became desperate. As eviction procedures were bound to prove lengthy, they decided to do it another way. The bailiff contacted a private detective firm, and while the police stood by as passive onlookers the detective and his gang forced an entrance to a house illegally occupied by a family with three children. Though the authorities were shocked by the hostile reaction to this incident in the press, there was no official condemnation of the hired thugs — a silent consent, in fact, to a repeat performance. Sure enough, the whole scene was repeated one month later, this time at six in the morning, and two families were booted out. In spite of all the intimidation, the campaign continued, and a week later three houses in Ilford were occupied. Squatters also moved into other London boroughs. The next time the eviction gang tried an onslaught, the inhabitants and their helpers were prepared with sticks and helmets, and warded off the attack. Shop steward committees of companies like Ford, Plessey and Kellogg lent a helping hand in the refurbishing of squatted properties. Meanwhile the movement had spread further afield, and was no longer restricted to empty houses. In Notting Hill the sale of two large properties to a speculator was sabotaged by squatters who participated in the bidding and sent the auction into chaos. In South London and office building was occupied for five days in protest against the construction of offices instead of homes. In Brighton, squatters took over houses which had been scheduled for demolition to make way for a parking lot. All these actions brought nothing but positive publicity for the squatters' campaign until a number of squatters were arrested in connection with a bomb attack on an army information centre. But even without this, public opinion was bound to change: as squatting became widespread, the media's sympathy for its goals quickly evaporated.

Resistance to the eviction of the Endell Street Squatters under the flag of the London Street Commune gave the press its chance to let rip against those bloody

Comic from the radical architects' magazine *Arse*, England, 1970. © *Arse*.

Comic from the 'Prague Spring', Czechoslovakia, 1968. © Verlag GMBH & Co.

hippies, always trying to get something for nothing.

By 1975, however, London was possibly the world's most be-squatted city. From 1970 on just about every sizable English town had its own radical local press which took an aggressive stance against local plans for redevelopment. Cartoon strips on the subject reprinted here appeared in papers such as 'Islington Gutter Press', 'Mole Express', and 'Ned Gate'.

Besides the local press, other action committees now appeared to represent other needy groups that had hitherto had no voice. Dissident psychiatrists and psychology students brought out a magazine for 'abnormal psychiatry', which drew attention to the plight of the institutionalized mentally ill. Another group that started to raise its voice was that of prisoners. Like the soldiers' movements already described, this type of organization grew up all over the Western world.

The Claimants Unions, however, were a typically English phenomenon: they too used hard-hitting graphics for propaganda. These Claimants Unions were created to fight for the rights of the growing number of unemployed. It was felt that the time was ripe for a left-wing organization for the unemployed, as this was a group particularly receptive to the propaganda of the rapidly growing Fascist movement.

A good example of the propagandist use of strips can be found in 'Street Comix', some ten examples of which were issued by Dave Webster in 1970. And one of the best, if not the most effective, strip of this kind was that produced in 1970 by the group Big Flame in Birmingham in response to the Industrial Relations Act, showing what the consequences of such an Act might be. Another strip published by the same group in 1974 indicates that they made the connection between the struggle in the cities and the struggle in the factories. A less eye-catching but perhaps more effective comic strip is that distributed to Vauxhall workers in 1973, which was dedicated to all those workers who needed psychiatric treatment to make them fit for work again.

Strip poster about property speculation, England, 1972. © *Mole Express.*

Anarcho-Syndicalist strip poster, England, 1972. © *Black and Red Outlook.*

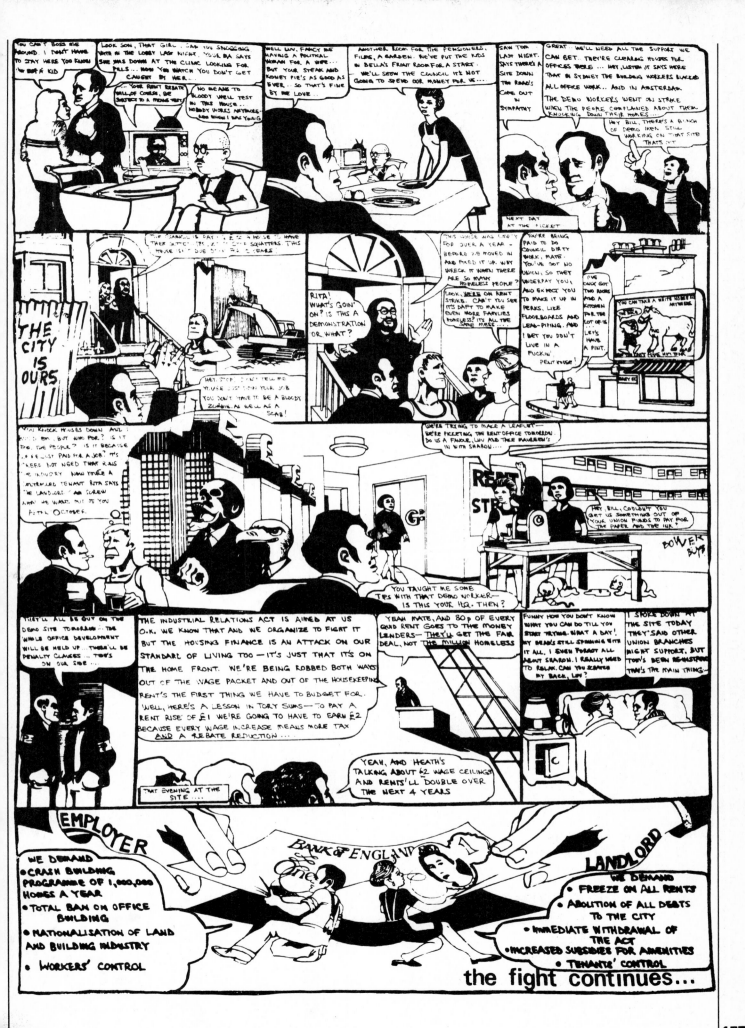

Page two of a comic about squatting, England, 1973.

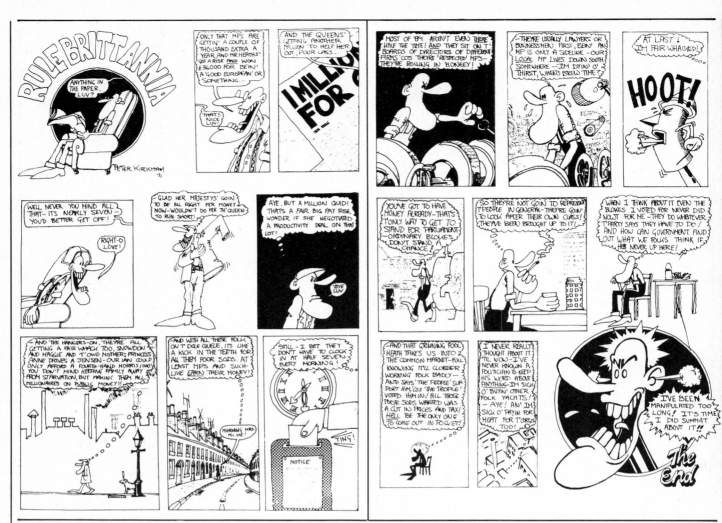

It wouldn't do for the Queen to run short, would it? England, 1971. © *Mole Express.*

Orchestrated politics, England, 1972. © *Seven Days.*

From *Case Con*, a magazine for radical psychologists, England, 1970. © *Case Con.*

Strip about a young woman who died unnoticed in gaol, England, 1972. © Hackney's People Press.

THEY CAME TO TAKE AWAY THE MANGROVE NINE BUT I DID NOTHING, COS I'M NOT BLACK

THEY CAME TO EVICT THE SQUATTERS BUT I DID NOTHING COS I'VE GOT A HOME

THEY CAME TO TAKE AWAY THE CLAIMANTS BUT I DID NOTHING COS I'VE GOT A JOB

THEY CAME TO TAKE AWAY THE PICKETS BUT I DID NOTHING COS I'M NOT ON STRIKE

THEY CAME TO TAKE AWAY THE STOKE NEWINGTON 8 BUT I DID NOTHING COS I'M NOT ANGRY

THEN THEY CAME TO TAKE ME AWAY AND THERE WAS NO ONE TO HELP

HELP!

Right: Solidarity is the answer, England, 1973. © *Islington Gutter Press.*

The scenario of this comic has been used so many times everywhere that it's impossible to determine where it came from. This adaptation is from England, 1969. © *The Black Dwarf*.

Claimants' comic, England, 1972.

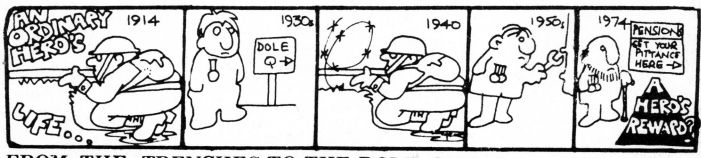

FROM THE TRENCHES TO THE DOLE QUEUF

From the *Strikers' Handbook*, England, 1971. © National Federation of Claimants' Unions.

Claimants' Union comic, England, 1975.

I GET THE IMPRESSION THAT IF THE FIRST GUY WAS CONTROLLING THINGS HE'D OPERATE ALONG SIMILAR LINES. DOESN'T SEEM TO BE MUCH CHOICE — DOES THERE ????

THE FRENCH HAVE A SAYING — "TO VOTE IS TO PISS AGAINST THE WIND," AND BETWEEN YOU AND ME, PALS, I THINK THEY'RE RIGHT.

DON'T BE MISLED BY "NEWS" BROADCASTS, AND ALL THE OTHER CRAP. "NEWS" IS WHAT YOU ARE TOLD. THEY DECIDE WHAT TO TELL YOU.

YOU ARE CONSTANTLY BEING CONDITIONED TO THINK WITHIN A NARROW FRAMEWORK. YOUR CREATIVE THOUGHT IS BEING SUPRESSED OR PERVERTED TO SERVE THE NEEDS OF CAPITALISM. YOU ARE BEING SUFFOCATED, AND SOME OF YOU MADE MENTALLY ILL BY THE MEANINGLESSNESS OF LIFE UNDER THIS SYSTEM. YOU HAVE NO GENUINE CHANCE TO CHANGE THE QUALITY OF YOUR LIFE THROUGH VOTING.

"Politics" IS A GAME. YOU DON'T HAVE TO PLAY IT THEIR WAY.

BECAUSE THEY MADE THE RULES.

Kick Back Comics in defence of three gaoled building workers, England, 1974. © Big Flame.

Pamphlet distributed in a Vauxhall Factory, England, 1973. © Mental Factory.

IN CASE YOU HAVEN'T REALISED IT, THIS COMIK HAS BEEN ABOUT ALTERNATIVE POLITICS, SOME OPTIONS TO CAPITALIST RELATIONSHIPS......
IN THE NEXT COMIK WE'LL BE SEEING THE COMMUNARDS PRODUCING POWER, HEAT AND LIGHT, BUILDING THEIR OWN HOUSES AND MAKING THEIR ARTIFACTS, CLOTHES AND OTHER NEEDS......
THE THIRD COMIK WILL SHOW THE COMMUNARDS GROWING AND PRODUCING FOOD, CELEBRATING THE HARVEST AND BUILDING THEIR BASIC ECONOMY

Four pages from *New Times*, a comic book by Cliff Harper, depicting a post-revolutionary situation, England, 1974. © Cliff Harper.

Poster about the proposed Industrial Relations Bill, England, 1970. © Big Flame.

HOT AUTUMN IN ITALY

The sit-in phenomenon really took off in Italy. The sweltering hot autumn of 1969 was remarkable for the spontaneous nature of innumerable strikes and occupations. It was the year in which the three-yearly wage agreements were up for renegotiation. But before the trade unions had had time to mobilize their members, the workers had taken matters into their own hands. A short strike by Fiat workers for example, in protest at the death of a worker during riots in Battipaglia, turned into a sit-in when the strikers refused to leave the factory. Tactics and strategies were used that were not in the trade-union handbook, but the unions had to go along with these to some extent in order not to lose control altogether. In the hope of buying industrial peace, the bosses gave in without much struggling to wage increases of up to 25 per cent. But they couldn't buy peace in the seething political climate, which was aggravated by Fascist violence. One of the Fascists' most notorious deeds was the bomb attack in Milan's town centre, in which sixteen people were killed: the anarchists got the blame. A kind of guerilla war sprang up in the factories, and the rate of acts of sabotage shot up.

The struggle was not confined to the factories, but spread to other sectors. When Milan town council tried to raise rents by 30 per cent, seven hundred families went on a rent strike. Evictions led to widespread riots. In May 1970 no less than five hundred policemen were called in to evict one family. Rent strikes and occupations became the most popular weapon for hitting back. In 1970 and 1971 innumerable houses were taken over by squatters in Milan, Turin and Rome. Another form of protest that was popular was the reduction of rent to a reasonable level by the tenant himself.

Strips and photo-strips especially have always been a very popular medium among the Italian working class. The main topic for the 'fumetti' (photo-strips) was, and still is, tortured love affairs in which women and men appear in cliché and conventional roles. An extreme example of a drawn version of this is 'Hessa', a super-Nazi who made an appearance in ludicrously large

Dutch edition of Hessa, neo-Fascist superwoman, Netherlands, 1970. © De Vrijbuiter.

editions for many years in several European countries.

In view of the popularity of these strips, it is surprising that the new revolutionary papers which were born in the 'Hot Autumn' made so little use of this medium. As in other Western countries, it was left to the more radical and Situationist groups in Italy to experiment enthusiastically with unorthodox design and comic strips.

Comic from *Science against the Proletariat*, Italy, 1973. © Stampa Alternativa.
1. The boss has promised to install air extractors next year.   2. The boss has *definitely* promised to install air extractors next year.

In Italy the work rate is the fastest of all of Europe, Italy, 1973. © Stampa Alternativa.
1. Can't you do something with your right foot as well?   2. Yes, this!

CRONACHE SINDACALI

From the satirical cartoon and comic magazine, *Ca Bala*, Italy, 1971. © *Ca Bala*.
1. 'Comrades, we've been striking too much now!'   'Now he's going to come out with his favourite proverb!!'   2. 'Remember: a struggle is a good thing as long as it's a short one.'

IL VENTOTTO FEBBRAIO SI APRE A SALERNO IL PROCESSO ALL'ANARCHICO GIOVANNI MARINI

The facts of the Marini case, Italy, 1974. © *Revista A*.

Gasparazzo, Italy, 1972. © *Lotta Continua*.

Facing pages: Donald Duck shows his true nature, Italy, 1970.
© *Lotta Continua*.

Donald Duck: the truth the bourgeois comics have repressed
1. 'Pity we are so busy at the University of Milan with the middle classes and Giovanni Marmotte's teachings...' 2. 'Damn middle-class kids!' 'This is the ideal place for an exciting anti-imperialist demonstration...' 3. (Daisy Duck: CPCI = Italian Communist Party) 'Darlings why do you look so sad? Election day draws near! And you will profit by it!' 'We want to organize an exciting anti-imperialist demonstration...' 4. 'In a working-class neighbourhood? Hmm — no. It would be better to stick up some posters explaining our demands. Leave that to me.' 5. In a working class slum, Donald struggles as usual to pay his bills. 'I've been given the sack because of my political activities. What shall I do?' 6. 'The only solution must be revolution!' 7. 'We need your vote to get our reforms through!' 'Well! you've certainly picked the right man!' 8. 'Just think about the value of resistance! You must participate in the struggle!' 'A cross on a voting paper? You call that a struggle?' 9. 'You talk like an extremist from *Lotta Continua*! Besides voting, you can also come along to an exciting anti-imperialist demonstration, with riots and all!' 'Dirty reformists!' 10. 'Dirty traitors! I'm off to the factory to demand my job back.' 10,000 used petrol coupons for sale. Inquiries to Agnellon degli Agnelloni (ennobled form of the name Agnelli, boss of FIAT). 11. Meanwhile, Agnellon degli Agnelloni is working. 'I have to enlarge the vault, because the profits of the Russian factory in Togliattigrad can't be fitted in any more' (reference to Togliatti, once head of Italian Communist Party). 12. 'Knock, knock — it's me, Donald Duck!' 'What? more demands?' 13. Donald's class hatred explodes: 'Listen to me, you dirty capitalist swine, you won't be here long! The people will destroy you!' 14. 'OUT! Damn anarchist extremist. I'll only talk to your shop steward. Don't you dare appear in my presence again!' 'We told you so! Come on, why don't you just vote and join in an anti-imperialist riot!' 15. 'Now I'm really on my own!' 16. 'I must rally the people! We must fight, a tough fight without fear...' 17. Donald organizes political activities in the factory and in the slums. 18. 'Comrades, the moment has come! We must fight capitalism, without fear!' 'My family and I are ready to fight Agnellon degli Agnelloni and the Communist Party's bureaucrats!' 19. News spreads like wildfire, the people organize themselves and arm themselves. 'At last! The bosses won't exploit us any longer! Long live the revolution!' 20. 'We're going to get rid of our exploiters! Bosses, bureaucrats, teachers...' 'Even union leaders, eh?' 21. 'Then we can finally be happy...' 22. And finally the bureaucrats realize what's going on. 'They are all standing armed to the teeth in the square and for you and me and the unionists all is finished!' 23. 'Damnation! The extremists are coming!' 24. After a long battle... 26. 'Come, comrades, we have earned all this with our own labour. Let's take it from that swine!' 27. No poverty and hunger any more, there is plenty for everyone. Gain is declared illegal. 28. 'Sob!' 'All my money gone! I'm a poor old bald bankrupt duck!' 29. 'We would have preferred an exciting...' '...anti-imperialist demonstration with riots and all that!' 'It's the end!'

PAPERINO

...QUELLO CHE I FUMETTI BORGHESI CI HANNO SEMPRE TACIUTO....

171

Hart's *BC* as used by Italian council Communists,
Italy, 1970. © Ludd.
1. 'The proletariat is always asleep. Thank goodness we of the unions are
here to help them voice their demands.' 2. 'Damn! He's woken up!' 'I
am your factory's shop steward and I've come to ask you for your
endorsement.' (Ballots). 'NO! The unions are only a tool to integrate us
into capitalist society!' 3. 'I told you he was a trouble maker.' 'He
needs to be taught a lesson.' 4. 'Swine!' 5. 'Leave it to me.' 6. Bal-
lot box. 7. 'CHAINS.' 8. 'I thought democracy had made them more
sensible!' 9. 'WATCH OUT because when *we* are in control, the power
of the workers' councils will mean an end to all power!'

Comic from the radical magazine *Le Streghe*, Italy, 1972. © *Le Streghe*.
1. 'The weapon of the critique cannot compete with... 2. the critique
of weapons...' 3. 'Material force... must be defeated by material force
but... 4. theory... 5. becomes material force... as soon as it takes hold
of the masses...' 6. 'Theory is able to take hold of the masses...
7. as soon as it manages to speak to the people directly and it...
8. speaks to the people directly as soon as it becomes... 9. radical... to
be radical means to get to the root of the question.' 10. 'But the root of
the question is man himself!'

declino e caduta del
movimento studentesco

Right: Situationist pamphlet on the student movement, Italy, 1969.
The decline and fall of the student movement. 'Look what's become of me
— all because I allowed myself to be led by the bureaucrats who wish to
"build up" the movement.' **THE PROLETARIAT HAS NOTHING TO
CONSTRUCT, ONLY TO DESTROY.**

VIOLENT VANGUARD

The Front de Libération de Québec, which fought for the rights of the large French minority in Canada, had started to use bombs to push home their arguments back in the early sixties. In 1969 a wing of the Liberation Front tried to blow up Montreal's stock exchange. American property also came under fire, and in 1970 a British diplomat and a minister of the State of Quebec were kidnapped. The authorities reacted by sending 7,000 federal troops to Montreal. Some 450 militant socialists were taken into custody.

The events in Canada are just one example of the politically motivated violence that spread in the sixties and seventies. Another example is the anarchist May 1 Movement which had been active throughout Europe since the mid-sixties in challenging the symbols of the Spanish dictatorship. The immediate motives might have been different, but the violence had grown out of the same underlying cause: the unbearable tension between the power of the state and the impotence of the people.

In Germany, during a visit to Berlin by the Shah of Persia on 2 June 1967, one of the demonstrators, a student called Benno Ohnesorg, was shot dead, and the following year there was an attempt on student leader Rudi Dutschke's life. Such incidents contributed to the growing radicalism of the German student movement. They led to violent demonstrations against the rightist Springer Press (which had for some time been conducting a campaign against the students) and to an intensification of protest in general. A group of extremists — Andreas Baader, Gudrun Ensslin, Thorwald Proll and Hans Sohnlein — set fire to a Berlin department store in protest against the war in Vietnam. On 14 May an armed group stormed the building where Baader was being held, and together with Ulrike Meinhof they escaped via East Berlin to Jordan, where they were trained in guerilla tactics by El Fatah. They returned to Germany under the name 'Rote Armee Fraktion'. Their first step was to carry out three bank raids in West Berlin within the space of half an hour. The deeds of the RAF, or the Baader-Meinhof gang, as they are popular known, provoked an increasingly repressive reaction from the authorities. Radical laws were introduced to combat terrorism but they also succeeded in strengthening the state's control over the people in whose name the terrorists were fighting. Although Germany's workers were also hardening in their approach to the authorities, the RAF was unable to cash in on this, and only succeeded in alienating the workers.

Elsewhere in Europe, however, a number of violent separatist movements did succeed in winning the support of the workers — for example, in Corsica, and in Spain's Basque country. Organized violence became a universal phenomenon: the guerillas in Latin America, Ulster's urban terrorists, the Palestine Liberation Movement. In America too, the students' frustration at the absence of real social change led to increasingly violent confrontations with the authorities. Protest against the Vietnam war took on the dimensions of a mass movement, but it was rewarded only with an invasion of Cambodia. A section of the SDS, which had named itself Weatherman, went underground at the end of 1969 in the hope of provoking a revolutionary situation by force. Very little time had passed before the FBI top ten wanted list was filled with the names of former SDS leaders like Mark Rudd and Bernadine Dohrn. New Left circles, which rejected the idea of violence, condemned them bitterly and even accused them of being Federal agents provocateurs. To give some idea of the extent of political violence in the USA, here are some figures taken from a survey on guerilla activity in America by the magazine 'Scanlan': 1965 witnessed 16 acts of terrorism; in 1966 it was 34; in 1967, 56; in 1968 it had risen to some 250; in 1969 to 503, and in 1970 to 546. Prime targets were government buildings, the offices of large corporations, police stations, military institutions and universities.

In England, the Angry Brigade appeared. In contrast to other urban guerilla groups, they represented neither a central party organization nor a vanguard ideology. This emerges from their seventh communiqué, in which they wrote, 'revolution is autonomous spontaneous action, we make it ourselves'. Further on in the same communiqué, they attacked the political parties for their insistence that the passive working class needs leaders from the middle class. Their own spectacular action, however, equally reduced the working class to indifference.

The urban guerilla's argument can be summed up as follows: 'Once you accept that the ruling classes will never renounce their privileges without a fight, and therefore that the revolution, when it comes, cannot take place without an armed struggle, then you must also accept that the time to act is now. When conditions have deteriorated to such an extent that the time is ripe for the bloodbath, there won't be any time for preparations, as together with the growing consciousness of the revolutionary classes goes a growth in repression.'

The romance of the avengers, Canada, 1973. © Georgia Straight.

Anti-IRA cartoon published by Ulster Unionists, Ulster, 1972. © *The Orange Cross.*

DANGER IMMÉDIAT.

THE **F.L.Q.** IS MENACING THE POPULATION !

(IT'S BEEN SAID, THUS IT MUST BE TRUE....)

BUT IS IT REALLY THE ONLY MENACE WHICH IS HANGING OVER QUEBEC ?

AS EVERYONE KNOWS, AT THE ONSET OF THE WAR MEASURES ACT ONE UNHAPPY SOLDIER WAS KILLED WHEN HE GOT TANGLED UP IN HIS GUN AS HE JUMPED FROM A TRUCK.

THUS, IF YOU'RE A MAN IN THE PUBLIC EYE: A TEACHER, A JOURNALIST, A WRITER, A TRADE UNIONIST, AN INTELLECTUAL, AS CAOUETTE MIGHT SAY — A RADICAL LIBERAL, AS SPIRO AGNEW MIGHT SAY — IN OTHER WORDS, IF YOU HAVE ABOVE AVERAGE INTELLIGENCE AND ARE CONSCIOUS OF THE POLITICAL AND SOCIAL PROBLEMS IN QUEBEC, YOU ARE A NUMBER ONE SUSPECT. HERE'S WHAT MIGHT HAPPEN TO YOU....

YOU WILL CERTAINLY BE SEARCHED — IN THE MIDDLE OF THE NIGHT !

A PLAINCLOTHESMAN WILL SHOW UP AT YOUR HOUSE ... ACCOMPANIED BY 40 SOLDIERS.

THUS, IF BY CHANCE AND BAD LUCK, YOUR LITTLE DOG BITES THE REAR END OF SOME SOLDIER ...!

IT'S REALLY TOO BAD... BUT IT WILL SAVE THEM FROM BEING JUDGED... WON'T CAOUETTE BE HAPPY!

TAKE THIS OTHER CASE, STILL MORE DRAMATIC... ONE DAY, SOME LITTLE GIRLS ARE GOING TO CHURCH WITH THEIR TEACHER ...

MEANWHILE, ON THE OTHER SIDE OF THE STREET, A SOLDIER IS SLOWLY MAKING HIS ROUNDS. SUDDENLY!

A LITTLE BANANA PEEL!

WHAT A CATASTROPHE !!!

OBVIOUSLY, IF THIS WERE TO HAPPEN IN THE TOWN OF MOUNT ROYAL, IT WOULD CURE THE PROBLEM OF THE FRENCH-SPEAKING CATHOLIC SCHOOL!

BUT IT'S IN YOUR AREA, IN YOUR OWN NEIGHBOURHOOD, ON YOUR OWN STREET, THAT SUCH A DRAMA MIGHT UNFOLD. ALL THIS BECAUSE OF THE WAR MEASURES IDIOCY... AND A BANANA PEEL. SO KEEP YOUR CITY CLEAN...

BUT YOU AIN'T SEEN NOTHING YET... NEXT WEEK I'LL SHOW YOU HOW THIS POOR PRIVATE WILL SET OFF, SINGLE-HANDEDLY AND UN-AWARES, A NATIONAL CATASTROPHE....

'What is the immediate threat to the people?', Canada, 1970. © **Quebec Presse**

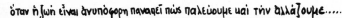

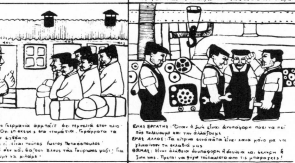

Comic made by Greek immigrant workers in Germany and illegally distributed in Greece, Germany, 1970.

When life becomes unbearable, we must fight to change it.

1. Thomas: 'You're all right there, Michalis, with your chestnuts! But let's be honest, I can't make a decent living in Saloniki. My life will begin in Germany. Within six months I'll have paid off my debts and then the land will be Irini's.' 2. Thomas: 'At last, in four hours it'll all be over, we're nearly in Frankfurt!' Angelos: 'Not so fast, friend. Your troubles are only beginning. I know what emigration means, from back in '58, the time of Karamanlis and Papandreou. Don't kid yourself!' 3. Foreman: 'In Deutschland immer Arbeit, work, work, no lazing in the sun. No visitors in the dormitories. Mail is distributed every Saturday.' Thomas: 'What a terrible man, just like Papadopoulos!!' Ismet: 'Why aren't all the Turks allowed in one dormitory? Are they afraid that we'd then be able to talk to each other?' 4. Worker: 'When life becomes unbearable we must fight to change it.' Second worker: 'All the unions do is grease the chains of our slavery.' Thomas: 'Yes, our work is unbearable and our life is hard! At least I can try to get out of these wooden barracks.' 5. Accommodation agency: No rooms to let for Greeks and Turks. 6. 'Who chose *them* as our representatives?' 'They're just like Brandt's union bullies.' 'What do they want? To kick out the American fascists, or

to enter parliament?' The People's Democratic Society: 'Listen to your representatives. The "Free World" will redress all injustices.' 7. Angelos: 'Mao teaches us not to be afraid of setbacks.' Worker: 'We'll all go together!!! He's robbing us of all our wages with his high rents! We must show that we're Greek labourers, not animals!' 8. Down with the bosses. We want better accommodation. Destroy the barracks. 10. My dear friend Michalis, I am well, I hope all is well with you too. I was wrong about life in Germany. It is true I earn a good wage, but I have to live in a concentration camp. We're not even allowed to piss during working hours in the factory. And in the evenings, in the barracks, we're isolated, as if we were in solitary confinement. I miss Greece, my family and friends. But I'm going on! All the Greeks here are in the same boat, as are all the other immigrants. Therefore we should change our lives altogether; we mustn't wait for one of us to take the initiative! And we shan't forget our fatherland. I embrace you, Thomas. 11. Hotel. Thomas: 'Here's your rent, dirty nazi! This is the foreigners' answer to your racist insults!' 12. Those who accept oppression and exploitation are slaves. We must not forget our brothers in Greece. We must continue to defend our rights, as we have just done. We won because we had the courage to hold our heads high and because we stood by each other, and acted as one man. KKE — Greek Communist Party in exile.

176 Surprise, surprise, France, 1972. © *Lutte Occitane.*

Anarchist comic after the execution of Puig Antich, England, 1974. © *Black Cross.*

THE PACIFIERS!

ATROCITY COMICS PROUDLY PRESENTS:

THE STORY OF AMERICA'S SEARCH FOR PEACE IN TROUBLED VIETNAM

Atrocity comics by Steve Gilbert, USA, 1970.

MARK RUDD was ...

"Ashamed to go to his class reunion!"

THIS CAN BE YOUR "BIG BREAK"

Part of the movement denounced Weathermen tactics and suggested their leaders were *agents provocateurs*, USA, 1970. © *Eyewitness.*

What happened to peace and love?, USA, 1971.

MADAME KY'S PUZZLE PAGE!

TRY THESE ON FOR SIZE, YANKEE PIG!

Mysteries of the East

**Featuring Riddles, Posers,
Brain Teasers, & Conundrums!**

1. Two Green Beret interrogators are hovering in a helicopter eleven thousand feet over Thuong Duc with a number of suspected Vietcong prisoners. The first interrogator can throw five suspected Vietcong prisoners from the helicopter in five seconds. The second interrogator can throw ten suspected Vietcong prisoners from the helicopter in ten seconds. Which interrogator can throw twelve suspected Vietcong prisoners from the helicopter in the shortest time?

2. On July 3, 1966, the *New York Times* reported: "United States Air Force lawyers made condolence payments of 33 piasters (about 30 cents) this weekend to each of the families of seven children killed accidentally by an Air Force weapon...."At this rate, how many piasters would the lawyers have to pay if a B-52 napalmed a South Vietnamese orphanage and wiped out 116 children?

3. *How many dead Vietcong can you find in this picture?*

Answers

1. The interrogator who throws five prisoners in five seconds takes 1¼ seconds between throws, since there are four intervals between the first and last throws. The other interrogator requires ten seconds for nine intervals, or 1⅛ seconds between throws. Therefore, the second interrogator will take less time to throw twelve suspected Vietcong prisoners from the helicopter—12⅜ seconds compared with 13¾ seconds. 2. Nothing at all! Since the children were orphans, they have no families to receive condolence payments, thus saving the U.S. taxpayer $34.80. 3. According to an official Pentagon body count, there are 381.

Ron Cobb cartoon, USA, 1970. © Ron Cobb/ Sawyer Press.

Comic from 'Fire', a magazine published by SDS at the Flint conference when Bernadine Dohn announced that she was going underground, USA, 1969. © SDS

182 'What is this crazy bastard up to anyway?', USA, 1969. © Willie Murphy.

Or can't you smell it any more?, USA, 1970. © Gary Ratto.

ATTENTION ALL REVOLUTIONARIES!

NOW YOU TOO CAN MAKE A BOMB! WIN FRIENDS! DESTROY BOURGEOIS PROPERTY! JUST FOLLOW THESE SIMPLE INSTRUCTIONS!

1. COP ABOUT A MILLION FIRE-CRACKERS...

2. ADD A MOTHER HUGE FUSE...

3. PLACE BENEATH CIA OFFICE, INDUCTION CENTER, ETC. ... LIGHT FUSE

4. RUN LIKE HELL...!

From a special pamphlet published after a bomb explosion wrecking a military research building in Madison, USA, 1970. © *Madison Kaleidoscope.*

what to do when THE FBI comes

IN THE WAKE OF THE CITY HALL BOMBING, the F.B.I. HAS BEEN MAKING VISITS TO MANY PEOPLE'S HOMES. THESE VISITS ARE AS MUCH FOR GENERAL PURPOSES OF INFORMATION GATHERING AS THEY ARE FOR APPREHENDING THE BOMBERS. TALKING TO THEM NOW WILL ONLY MAKE THEIR JOB OF INTIMIDATION + REPRESSION EASIER IN THE FUTURE!

TALK, PUNK, OR ELSE WE KNOW YOU'RE GUILTY!

THEY MAY COME ON **TOUGH**...

WE'RE HERE TO MAKE SURE YOU'RE NOT INVOLVED, OLD BUDDY.

THEY MAY COME ON **FRIENDLY**...

HOW'S THAT CORN ON YOUR LEFT BIG TOE DOING, NICK?

OR AS IF THEY ALREADY KNOW A LOT

THEY MAY PLAY DUMB AND TEMPT YOU TO TRY TO OUTSMART THEM...

DUH...

IT IS A FEDERAL CRIME TO LIE TO THEM!

THERE IS ONLY **ONE** SAFE, LEGAL RESPONSE YOU SHOULD MAKE:

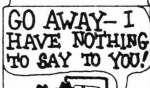

GO AWAY— I HAVE NOTHING TO SAY TO YOU!

SLAM

THEY MAY TELL YOU TO CALL YOUR LAWYER—THIS IS A TRICK—IGNORE THEM! DO NOT LET THEM IN YOUR HOUSE IF THEY DON'T HAVE A WARRANT. THEY MAY REMAIN ON YOUR DOORSTEP OR POUND ON YOUR WINDOWS... IGNORE THEM. THEY HAVE MORE TRICKS THAT AREN'T LISTED HERE—FOLLOW THE ONE BASIC RULE: **DON'T TALK TO THE F.B.I.!**

Don't talk to the FBI, USA, 1971. © *Quicksilver Times.*

Watch the company goons, USA, 1970. *Madison Kaleidoscope.*

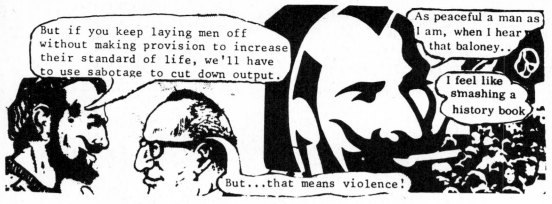

Greetings from your friendly neighbourhood anarchist, England, 1972. © *Black and Red Outlook.*

the Barnet Brigade

Comic about the team of policemen that caught the Angry Brigade, England, 1971. © *Strike.*

SABOTAGE

MOLOTOV COCKTAIL– A BOTTLE IS FILLED WITH 2/3 GAS AND 1/3 OIL. A FUSE IS INSERTED AND THE BOTTLE CORKED. THE FUSE IS LIGHTED AND THE BOTTLE HURLED AT OBJECTIVE ON BREAKING THE CONTENTS WILL IGNITE. THE ENEMY WILL BE UNABLE TO EXTINGUISH IT WITH WATER.

TO SET A FIRE

A LIGHTED CIGARETTE IS PLACED IN A BOOK OF MATCHES AND LEFT ON COMBUSTIBLE MATERIAL.

HAND GRENADES:

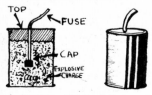

A FUSE OF 5 OR 6 SECONDS LENGTH IS INSERTED INTO A CAN FILLED WITH DYNAMITE AND SCRAPS OF IRON, NAILS, SCREWS, ETC.

From General Bayo's '150 questions for a guerrilla', USA, 1963. © Robert K. Brown.

CONSPIRACY?

Comic published by the Stoke Newington Eight Defence Group, England, 1972.

Comic by Willem made for Amsterdam's Nieuwmarkt Neighbourhood, Netherlands, 1972.

1. 'I love Amsterdam. It's a pity, though, that people still seem to be living there.' 'Yes, it's a shame really.' 2. 'They make it filthy and slow down the traffic.' 3. 'They confuse everything , they prattle and complain.' 'And they have bad breath!' 4. 'They occupy land which could be put to much more lucrative use.' 5. 'Amsterdam would be the most prosperous city in the world if only it had no residents!' 6. 'Can't we do something about it?' 7. 'We'll have to get them out!' 'We could gas them out with stink factories.' 8. Not much later… 'Cough, cough, hey, what does that factory produce?' 'Nothing, only bad smells. If you don't like it you can always leave.' 9. 'The plan has passed our wildest expectations: nobody is staying!' 'We can start to demolish the residential areas this afternoon.' 'Hack, cough — fresh air!' 10. 'The traffic hasn't flowed so easily in years!' (Police) 'Get out!'

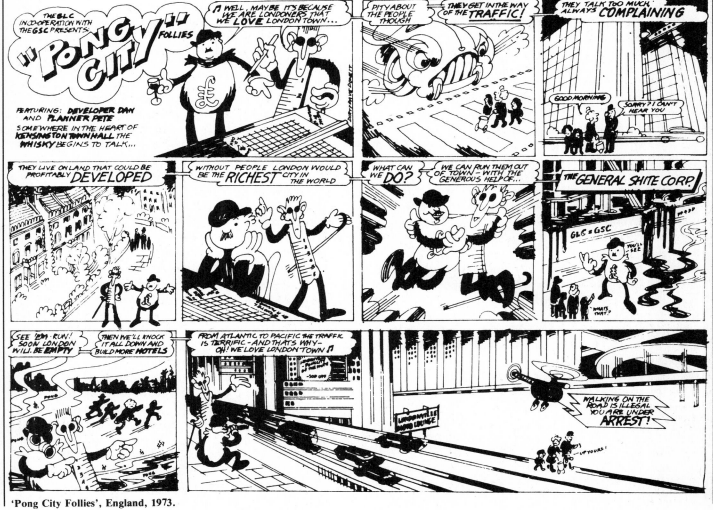

'Pong City Follies', England, 1973.

WE LIVE HERE AND WE'RE STAYING HERE

In all large cities, be it in Greece, Japan, America, England or Holland, the residential and living environment is being sacrificed to the demands of capital. In one city, residential areas are demolished to make way for offices, hotels or luxury flats; in another, the residents are tidied away to make room for motorways, roundabouts or some other planners' whim. The same old story is repeated everywhere. Different cities have different problems, different bottlenecks, but the fight is directed at the same enemy. To illustrate this, look at the strip created by Willem for the Amsterdam Nieuwmarkt Action Group. It was adopted without many changes in Strasbourg as well as in London.

At the end of the sixties, houses in the Nieuwmarkt district in Amsterdam were scheduled for demolition to make way for a new metro and motorway through the area. At the instigation of the Communist Party of the Netherlands (CPN) some of the residents set up a reorganization committee to support those among them who had to leave to make room for the new metro. Against the general wishes of the committee, squatters moved into a number of properties in the area. In 1969, some members of the committee broke away from the Communist Party and launched an action campaign to save the neighbourhood. A journalist living in the district started publishing a weekly magazine reporting on the progress made. His magazine, 'Lastage', was amalgamated a few months later with the rather sporadic 'Bethanienniews'. The new paper was called 'Niewsmarkt' ('Newsmarket'). When the older residents realized how successfully the squatters were renovating their houses in this run-down area, and therefore improving the whole neighbourhood, their sympathy with the squatters grew, and the whole district started to hum with activity. The construction of the metro was sabotaged: surveyors' instruments disappeared into the canals, and the municipal information booth went up in flames. Hundreds of people turned up at the meetings held by the Nieuwmarkt action group.

A pirate radio station was launched, Radio Sirene, which broadcast illicitly when the need arose. Many people did move out of the district, and accepted alternative accommodation from the council, but the newly vacated houses were immediately re-occupied by new squatters. Towards the end of 1974 the situation became critical, but the resistance of the action group had become better organized and was getting wide support. Residents agreed to contribute to a communal kitty, and the money was used to fix up buildings in a bad state of repair and to finance a more effective propaganda drive. A torrent of posters and pamphlets poured down on Amsterdam, and Nieuwmarkt delegations were sent to other action groups all over the country to seek support and solidarity.

The tension escalated and when a debate on the metro's future was held for the 'n'th time by the town council, an overwhelming vote in favour of its completion resulted, with the support of the building workers' union and the right-wing parties. Rioting and mass demonstrations ensued to 'save Amsterdam and begin with Nieuwmarkt'. In December 1974, when the council unexpectedly tried to render a recently vacated house in the area uninhabitable, demolition men were driven out and roof tiles were sent flying into the streets below, forcing the police, who had been called in, to beat a hasty retreat.

And now the evictions started in earnest. The inhabitants prepared to defend themselves: steel plates were bought with communal funds to make the ground floors impenetrable, and a suspension bridge was hung from steel cables over the twenty-metre-wide canal fronting the condemned houses. The raid occurred on 24 March. The defenders held out for a few hours, but then the police broke through the barricades in an armoured car. Using water-guns and tear-gas, the police succeeded in gaining possession of all the houses to be cleared, but demonstrations and clashes with the police continued all day throughout the city.

A fortnight later came the demolition of the last of the houses. With the motto 'prevent the authorities' violence with your presence', the action group organized a night watch. Almost a thousand police were needed in the early hours to smash the night-watchers' resistance. They finally succeeded in forcing their way into the occupied houses. Defenders were arrested, but in retaliation a building belonging to the subway

ER WAS EENS, WAT JE ZOU KUNNEN NOEMEN EEN OVERBLUF-SEL VAN WAT VROEGER EEN BOOM WAS. ER ZAT GEEN GROEN BLAADJE MEER AAN. DAT KWAM OMDAT DE WEZENS DIE ER IN WOONDEN DE BOOM "GETECHNOLOGISEERD" HADDEN. (DIT IS EEN MOEILIJK WOORD, MAAR HET HEEFT TE MAKEN MET WELVAART.) DE BOOM WAS ER AAN DOOD GEGAAN. ZOUWEN DE VIEZE WOLKEN, DIE ER OMHEEN HANGEN, DE LIJKLUCHT ZIJN?

contractors was occupied, and secret equipment stolen. Elsewhere in the city there were numerous sit-ins. But the big confrontation was over, although the action group continued its fight against the demolition of the neighbourhood, and new houses were occupied.

Out of this grass-roots struggle of resistance against demolition and rehousing which fought tooth and nail, and which inspired action groups in other cities and districts of Amsterdam, came many superb graphics. There was of course no shortage of comic strips, which appeared practically every week in the Nieuwmarkt local papers to illustrate the background of the struggle. The action committee even published its own comic magazine, 'Metropool'. It was created by professional artists living in the district as well as by amateurs, united in the threat of demolition. At a later stage, when Nieuwmarkt had become a national issue throughout Holland, other artists who did not live there also thronged to contribute to the stream of propaganda to show their solidarity. One such artist was Joost Swarte, who had started his own comic-strip paper, 'Modern Papier', in Eindhoven in 1971. This was one of the first Dutch underground comic-strip magazines, and it was followed by another, less critical paper, 'Tante Lenny'.

The struggle in other neighbourhoods also inspired exciting strips: another action committee published a comic about a four-lane motorway that had been planned to cut through their neighbourhood: it was drawn by a ten-year-old resident. The Banstraat in Amsterdam also had its share of property speculation: a few residents therefore got together to record the story in strip serial form. Every week the local residents could find another sheet with the continuing story of speculation in the Banstraat on the counters of the local shops.

In Utrecht a political comic-strip paper, 'Stripje', appeared for several years, directed at working youth. The more established commercial Dutch cartoonists working on children's comic weeklies revealed at a communal exhibition of their work in 1970 that they too could show political commitment. They published 'Wordt Vervolgd' as a one-off publication, but shortly afterwards these studio artists found themselves working together again on another protest cartoon-strip paper,

'De Vrije Ballon'. Robert van der Kroft was one of these artists who managed, despite his commercial commitments, to find time to work for action groups. See for example his excellent strips created for the 'Bajeskrant' (a paper for prison inmates).

As we have seen, the boundary between professional and amateur design becomes vague and irrelevant in the committed comic strip. Yet at the beginning its use was restricted to a particular artistic environment. Today, however, its use is becoming more universal. Self-made strips are used in industrial disputes, in strikes and occupations. The comic strip is in its heyday, it is used by political parties, in banks and offices, by progressives and conservatives, by the vanguard and the rearguard, by people who want to change their own lives as well as by people who want to change the lives of others.

I end the book with two illustrations showing the wide use that has been made of political comic strips. The first was made by Surinamers (from the former Dutch colony) and it shows the results of colonial and capitalist exploitation. The crowning sensation, the last strip, is the cover of Marx's 'Capital' in comic strip form.

This book has attempted to show political strips as the expression of a political consciousness that has manifested itself in different forms of resistance against 'the system' over the last ten to fifteen years. This resistance against the authoritarian structure of society is at the same time a struggle of control over our own lives. The comic strip, whether it has been clumsily scribbled or whether it has just been pasted together, is your opportunity to express yourself. You need no longer be put off by the cult of excellence and specialization which dominates every form of our culture. This is demonstrated by the new action and resistance movements which keep bubbling up from the bottom of our hierarchical society, and which are so forcefully illustrated by the strips reproduced in this book, especially in the most clumsy and childishly fashioned examples. To break out of the passive role assigned to us by society is a creative act. If you want things to get better, you'll have to work yourself at making them better. Your go.

OSLO FOR FOLKET

Oslo for the people, Norway, 1971. © Futurum Forlag.

High above Oslo our hero moves...
'How this makes me MAD.' 'Progress weakens my superpowers.' 'When we join the EEC I'll be outclassed by Italian and German superheroes.' 'The rent has just gone up, and I need new underwear. It can't go on like this.' 'I must join forces with all the others who want to destroy capitalism for once and for all.'
THE WORLD LIBERATION FRONT

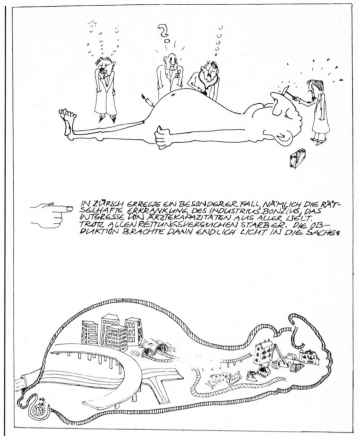

Anti-town-planning cartoon, Switzerland, 1974.
A strange thing has happened in Zurich: the mysterious illness of the industrialist Bonzius. Despite the care and attention of many specialists, he has died. An autopsy has revealed the cause of death.

Facing page: Comic about speculation, Netherlands, 1974.
© Beienhaas Productions.

Here starts the terrible Banstreet story — written with the hard facts!
1. Let's go back in time! In Banstreet, on the spot on which the playground now stands, stood a Roman Catholic school. It is 5 February, ten o'clock in the morning, the start of a normal working day...   2. 'We are the nuns, the owners of the land in Banstreet on which stands a school...   3. which we must close through a shortage of Catholic children. Therefore we wish to sell it.'   4. 'The name is Pas, sob-stuff property is the name of my game...   5. Thanks to my connections with the KRO Catholic TV/radio network dating from before the war, I know that there is an empty school for sale, with adjoining land in Banstreet. Though I have no money, I know someone who has access to it (and I know the nuns don't know that).'   6. 'My name is Caransa, Maupie to my friends, and I deal in...   7. anything that brings in money. Like a true Amsterdammer I know a great deal about my city. I hear that Mr Pas knows of some land that could prove useful to a property developer — and I know of just such a man!'   8. 'I am van der Meyden, and I remain behind the scenes...   9. I am a good friend of Maupie's. I am a builder and specialize in large profitable projects. I am certainly not the cheapest builder around, but there are other ways and means to attract custom...'   10. 'Lunch time! Thank goodness...because it is hard work, being a town councillor.'
1. 'I think a lot about Amsterdam's future, because I have just come back from a study-trip to America. What they've got over there — it's fantastic!   2. That's what Amsterdam should become — a real city, Europe's business heart.   3. Of course that can't be achieved overnight. Big business imposes certain conditions: modern office buildings, good access roads, parking space etc.   4. Naturally we are responsible for providing the access roads. As these are non-profit-making, they'll have to be paid for out of taxes... The investors themselves will take care of the offices and hotels.'   5. 'We work at Philips. Many other people work there... we have to think of our retirement. In this day and age, the normal old-age pension is no longer enough, and that's why we put a little extra by each month...   6. in the Philips Pension Fund. Naturally we have to make sure that our money doesn't lose its value over the years.'   7. 'I am Philips.'
1. 'And as employer I am naturally not afraid to take the responsibility for that money because...   2. Hello, can't you read that I'm busy?   3. ...because... it is always most profitable to speculate with that kind of big money!   4. It is useful to be able to see into the future in order to find projects which Philips knows will escalate in value, but...   5. ...it is better still to have friends in high places who can give you information. The nice thing about speculating with this money is that in the end the risk is ultimately carried by the workers... hi hi hi.   6. My friend Maupie Caransa is one of those people who has advance inside knowledge...   7. about good deals: roads, underground, the line out to the airport, parking lots etc...   8. What...   9. Who the hell is that ringing again????!!!'   10. (Artist) 'and shortly this story will be continued... truth is often worse than fantasy.'
To be continued.

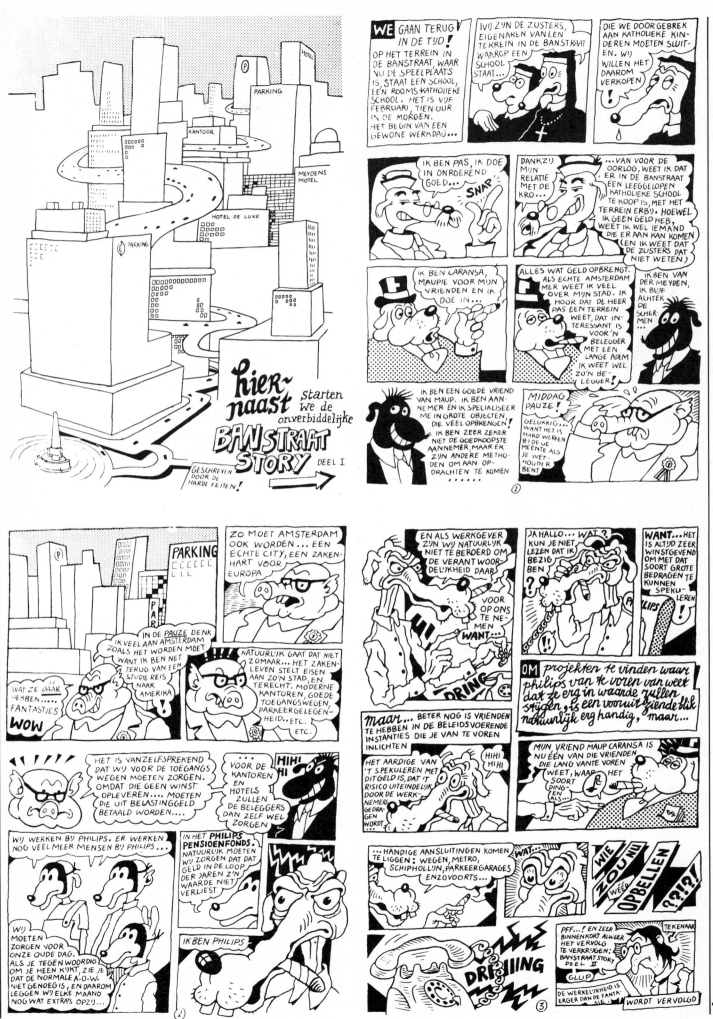

ÅR 1970 GAV DOM UT EN PLAN ENLIGT VILKEN DEN ARMA MÄLARDROTTNINGEN SKULLE TVÅNGSMATAS I ALDRIG SKÅDAD OMFATTNING DE NÄRMSTA ÅREN — ETT VÅLDFÖRANDE PÅ DEN STACKARS KVINNAN SOM HON KNAPPAST SKULLE ÖVERLEVA. MEN DÅ VAR MÅTTET RÅGAT. FRÅN ALLA HÅLL KOM KRAV ATT BIRGER JARLSKA KVINNOFRIDEN OCKSÅ SKULLE GÄLLA MÄLARDROTTNINGEN,

VID MITTEN AV 1200TALET GRUNDLADE BIRGER JARL STOCKHOLM SAMT INSTIFTADE FRIDSLAGARNA, BLAND DEM DEN OM KVINNOFRID. SNART GAVS STADEN NAMNET MÄLARDROTTNINGEN, TACK VARE SITT BEHAGFULLA YTTRE DÄR HON LÄTTJEFULLT VILADE VID MÄLARENS MYNNING.

ÄNNU VID MITTEN AV 1800TALET VAR HON EN SLANK OCH VACKER KVINNA, OM ÄN FATTIG. MEN INDUSTRIALISMEN UTNYTTJADE HENNE HÄNSYNSLÖST OCH PROPPADE MED ÅNGANS OCH ELEKTRICITETENS HJÄLP I HENNE SÅ MYCKET ATT HENNES FORMER BÖRJADE BLI BETÄNKLIGT RUNDA.

VID MITTEN AV VÅRT ÅRHUNDRADE VAR HON EN STORVUXEN OCH KORPULENT KVINNA, MED ANDNÖD OCH SVÅRA CIRKULATIONS-RUBBNINGAR. MEN MÄNNEN SOM VAR SATTA ATT FÖRVALTA ARBETET FRÅN BIRGER JARL OCH SKÖTA HENNES VÄL OCH VE, DOM LÅTSADES OM INGENTING.

Protest against urban developers, Sweden, 1970. © *Almbladet*.

THE DEVELOPMENT GIRL: THE QUEEN OF MÄLAR

1. Birger Jarl founded Stockholm in the mid thirteenth century and made laws to ensure peace, including laws to protect women's rights. Soon the city became known as the 'Queen of Mälar' because of her attractive setting at the mouth of the Mälar. 2. Despite her poverty, she was, until the mid nineteenth century, a slim and beautiful lady. But the industrial revolution took advantage of her and stuffed her with steam and electricity until she was decidedly plump. 3. By the middle of this century she was a fat and corpulent dame with serious respiratory and circulation problems. But the men who had been appointed to supervise her welfare and Birger Jarl's work acted as if nothing was wrong. 4. 'No, please, I simply cannot take another million.' 'Yes, come on, one more mouthful for Järva (new suburb)...' 'And then another for Botkyrka...' 'And one for Nacka...'

In 1970 they put forward a plan to fatten the poor Mälar Queen to unimaginable proportions, an assault the poor woman would barely survive. But that was the last straw. From all sides it was demanded that Birger Jarl's rights for women should also protect the Mälar Queen.

For whom is the city being planned?, Germany, 1971.
© *Lehel Zeitung.*
DEMOCRACY, AND NEVERTHELESS…
1. The Lehel citizens protest… Lehel for the Lehelers. Down with high rents!

2. Then… (Town council) '…we hereby declare that Lehel will stay a residential area… 3. …several years later… 'For sale — four-room homes, from DM194,900.' 'To let! two-room flats, from DM500.' 'And this is the last of the original residents of Lehel.'

Ghent cartoon later adapted in Antwerp, Belgium, 1973.
1. Finally they are going to ask the little man's opinion… 2. about their plans to build… 3. motorways and… 4. 'Good morning, sir. We'd like your opinion on the proposal to build a motorway here…'

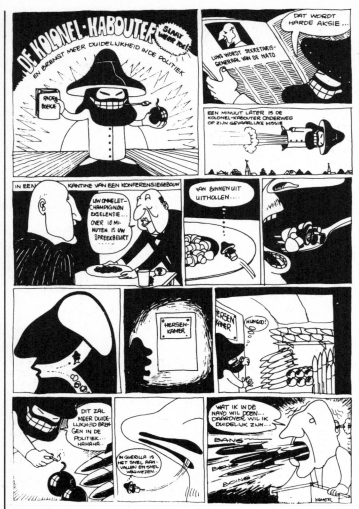

From the *Kabouter-Kolonel*, paper of a more extreme wing in the Kabouter movement, Netherlands, 1971.
1. Colonel Gnome strikes again! and makes politics more easy to understand. 2. Luns appointed Secretary-General of NATO. 'This means action…' 3. One minute later, Colonel Gnome is on his way on his dangerous mission. 4. In the canteen of the conference centre: 'Your mushroom omelet, excellency…It'll be your turn to speak in ten minutes.' 5. 'Attack the hollow core…' 8. Brain room. 9. 'My God!' 10. 'This will bring greater understanding to politics…ha, ha, ha.' 11. 'In guerilla warfare, attack must be swift, and withdrawal must be swifter…' 12. 'I want to make quite clear what I intend to do in NATO …BANG!'

What to expect of the housing authorities, Netherlands, 1972.
© Bert Griepink.
1. '…the housing shortage, which we, as experts and interested parties, are responsible for solving, with pragmatic ruthlessness…' 'I'm not bothered!' 'Yawn.' 'Housing shortage? Exaggerated!' 2. '…um…that is to say, ruthless analysis. What's the crux of the problem? Right: the impatience of the so-called homeless! Which leads to the undermining of the PROFITS of bonafide property builders and speculators…' 'Squatters?' 'Group sex…' 'DRUGS!' 3. 'This undermining of our capitalistic consumer economy must be fought tooth and nail by replacing those districts where houses are illegally occupied with motorways and banks…' 'Communists?' 'Rents there are much too low anyway.' 'Troublemakers!' 4. '…and to demolish them. The need however to find alternative accommodation for all these people brings us back to the problem of the housing shortage. For which, we, as interested parties …um, blah, blah, blah…' 'Clap clap.' 'Yawn.' 'Hear, hear!'

Facing page: Dutch Kabouter comic. The Kabouters (gnomes) were a group of anarchist-inspired young people who had partly come out of the Provo movement and called for an amiable revolution. Netherlands, 1970.
1. Once upon a time there was what you could call the remains of a tree. Not a single green leaf remained on its branches. That was because the beings that lived in it had 'technologized' it (this is a difficult word, but it has to do with prosperity). Perhaps the filthy clouds that hung above it were the fumes of death… 2. One fine day, it so happened that a new form of life was born to the old rotting tree stump: small mushrooms which fed on the juices of the rotting wood. If you looked closely, you could see they were…gnomes! 3. The gnomes saw large creatures driving round in great big tin cans which let off stinking farts. They decided to ask why they did this… 4. The large creatures answered friendlily: 'I think it's luxurious' (difficult word, has to do with prosperity). 'I'm pleased mine's a bigger one.' 'Mine is all nice and shiny.' 5. The gnomes called a meeting to discuss these ideas. The subject under discussion was the filthy sputtering of engines. 6. They did not believe that deliberate foul play was involved. After exhaustive discussions, they discovered that it was all due to technical shoddiness. 7. They set to work. 'This is the solution!' 8. At night, the industrious little people set out to rectify the faults of the motor-cans. 'Fixed!' 9. The next day: results were beyond all their wildest expectations. Not only had the fumes and sputtering stopped, but it appeared that the big beings had also decided to give up their aggressive driving.

ER WAS EENS, WAT JE ZOU KUNNEN NOEMEN EEN OVERBLIJF-SEL VAN WAT VROEGER EEN BOOM WAS. ER ZAT GEEN GROEN BLAADJE MEER AAN. DAT KWAM OMDAT DE WEZENS DIE ER IN WOONDEN DE BOOM "GETECHNOLOGISEERD" HADDEN. (DIT IS EEN MOEILIJK WOORD, MAAR HET HEEFT TE MAKEN MET WELVAART.) DE BOOM WAS ER AAN DOOD GEGAAN. ZOUWEN DE VIEZE WOLKEN, DIE ER OMHEEN HANGEN, DE LIJKLUCHT ZIJN?

OP EEN GOEDE DAG GEBEUR-DE HET. OP DE OUDE ROT-TENDE BOOMSTRONK ONT-STOND NIEUW LEVEN IN DE VORM VAN KLEINE PADDE-STOELEN DIE ZICH VOED-DEN MET DE SAPPEN UIT HET VERGANE HOUT. ALS JE GOED KEEK WAREN HET ... KABOUTERS!

DE KABOUTERS ZAGEN GROTE WEZENS IN VIEZE-WINDEN LATEN-DE BLIKKEN RONDRIJ-DEN, EN BESLOTEN HEN TE VRAGEN WAAROM ZE DAT DEDEN ...

DE GROTE WEZENS ANT-WOORDEN VRIENDELIJK

IK VIND HET LUXUEUS*

IK VIND HET FIJN DAT HIJ GROTER IS

DE MIJNE GLIMT

* MOEILIJK WOORD, HEEFT TE MAKEN MET WELVAART

OM DEZE INDRUKKEN TE VERWERKEN GINGEN DE KABOUTERS VERGADEREN. ONDERWERP VAN GESPREK WAS HET VIEZE MOTERGEKNETTER

ZE GELOOFDEN NIET DAT ER BOZE OPZET IN HET SPEL WAS. NA DIEPGAANDE STUDIE ONTDEKTEN ZE DAT HET HIER EEN TECH-NIESE SLORDIGHEID BETROF.

ZE TOGEN AAN HET WERK

DIT IS DÉ OPLOSSING

'SNACHTS TROK HET NIJVERE VOLKJE ER OP UIT OM HET EUVEL AAN DE MOTER-BLIKKEN TE VERHELPEN.

GEFIKST

DE VOLGENDE MORGEN: HET EFFECT WAS BOVEN VERWACHTING, WANT TEGELIJK MET HET OPHOUDEN MET HET WALMIKNET-TEREN, BLEKEN DE WEZENS OOK HET AGRESSIEVE RIJDEN TE HEBBEN OPGEGEVEN.

195

Election pamphlet of the Pacifist Socialist Party, Netherlands, 1974.
1. PSP list 7 — taken from our programme: 2. The consolidation of working and living: firms must be forced to be located where workers live. 3. Money hitherto spent on the construction of motorways will be spent on improving public transport. 4. Pollution prevention is better than paying for it. The reclamation of the Markerwaard should be dropped. 5. Preventive health: nutritional and dental care instead of the makeshift options like the fluoridation of drinking water. 6. You can receive the full PSP programme by paying 1 guilder into Giro account....

Facing page: German Kabouter comic, Germany, 1971. © Heinzelpress.
HEINZ THE GNOME
1. The golden rays of the dawning sun creep into Heinz's home. Groggy with sleep he rises from his bed. 2. 'Yawn. Well, I might as well potter along and wash.' 3. 'Phew, that stinks of carbolic acid.' 4. 'Filthy, mucky Rhine.' It is the sixth time that week that Heinz is unable to wash himself. He begins to think... 5. His stomach rumbles...He looks for berries and mushrooms. But his natural instinct warns him off... 'Aha, I knew it, DDT.' 6. 'But am I the only one to notice it?' 7. 'NO.' 'Hey, look, it's Joachim the gnome.' 8. 'The Gnomes and I, we'll manage to pull through...' 9. Will the Gnomes and Heinz manage? What is happening behind their small backs? Wait for the next instalment!

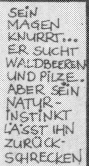

The fall of the vulture, Netherlands, 1972.

1. Vulture! The dictionary defines it as a merciless hungry bird or person of prey. But there's more to it than that, as we shall see... 2. All ties are severed... 'We'll plague them until they leave the old neighbourhoods... and drive them into the expensive dormitory suburbs!' 3. The left-wing political parties who call the tune in Amsterdam have changed, over the years, from being capitalism's worst enemies to being its slaves. Under the guise of cleaning up the inner-city slums and building garden suburbs, they have managed to free the valuable land of the inner city, destroying the integrity and unity of the working-class neighbourhoods. With the building of the dormitory-ghettoes (presented as garden suburbs) came large industrial estates, shopping centres, university campuses and office buildings. This division of work and residential areas led to ever-increasing transport problems, and bureaucracy and technocracy thrived at the expense of the residents and workers. Traffic, hence also public transport, became heavily congested. 4. Even the underground, which is meant to link the dispersed living and working districts outside Amsterdam, only makes the problem worse. With all those hordes of people travelling underground, car traffic will completely take over streets and roads, and more great big buildings will be erected on the sites of the underground entrances — more demolition! (face:) This is you! (sign:) 25 years red. 25 years housing shortage. City management becomes more and more sophisticated, and the city becomes more and more uninhabitable. Work and transport planned down to the last penny, and the journey between home and work keeps growing longer. Holidays and leisure time become increasingly packaged, and people become more lonely. 'The only fair rent is *no* rent!' 'But the good of the community is only served if everybody participates in its management...' 'As the rot spreads, ideas about change grow in those who suffer...' 5. Residents occupy the neighbourhood: (Police: 'We'd better get out of here!') 'We'll take what we want!' 'Self rule!' 6. Workers occupy the factories: 'Production but not greed for profit!' 'We're the only ones who can still stop pollution!' 'This is just the beginning...'

Suburban nightmare in Metropool, Netherlands, 1972. © Albert Blitz.
1. THE SUBURBS…ghastly tumours on the city's overflow roads.
2. Where the electric sockets in the concrete indicate where the economy's interesting acquisitions are meant to be placed… 'Drop of coke, Gladys?'
3. The plastic dream… 4. The dream created by the Great Citizen for the little citizen… 'This space could be used for at least 500 homes!' 'When I was a young architect I would have protested, resisted…'
5. 'But if I say no now I won't get the contract, nor the next contract… and then I'll be broke, and then they'll send in the bailiffs!' '…with parking space, otherwise not enough cars will be sold!' 'Yes, I'll do it!!' 6. The last glint of light that still manages to penetrate the smog shines wanly on the already crumbling concrete jungle…

Joost Swarte on the Amsterdam metro, Netherlands, 1972, © Joost Swarte.

Frankenstein's Underground.
1. 'I'm in a position to breathe new life into public transport thanks to the loans I've been able to obtain at very favourable terms.' 2. 'Who is lending you that money, Dr Frankenstein?' 'Shut up, you ugly creep! You're here to work, not to ask questions!' 3. 'Besides, don't you hear that banging on the door? Go and open up, stupid.' 'Groan!' 4. Bang, bang. 'Coming, coming.' 5. 'Let us in — we've come to see Dr Frankenstein.' 'Ah gentlemen, come in.' 6. 'Go away and play somewhere.' 7. 'Listen Frankenstein, you mustn't let financial problems come in the way of your Underground project! Do come and ask us for more money if you need it. You understand, of course, that when the inner city collapses as a result of your subterranean burrowing we'll take over to build our new office complexes!' 'I knew it, you can never trust your master.'

On the Amsterdam metro, commentary by an action group in Strasbourg, France, 1974. © Bernard Holtrop.

1. Amsterdam, summer 1974. For several years now the authorities have been destroying old neighbourhoods to make room for a new underground. 'Shit! We've got it wrong again! It's costing us five times more than we calculated originally...' 'Fool!' 2. 'It's a disaster! But this cursed underground has already cost us too much to stop building it now...' 3. 'Let's hope that one day it'll be profitable.' 'But of course! Nothing could be easier, we promise you.' 4. Plans for a new underground are also being prepared in Strasbourg... 5. 'The city must be planted full of offices, banks, etc..., and the population must be shifted to the suburbs: the subway will be crowded every day with people commuting to work.' 'I forbid you to break up the whole old part of the city to build skyscrapers!' 6. In the meantime, one building after another is sold and is left empty, despite the housing shortage. 'It's a scandal!' 'It's empty! Let's take it over and squat.' 7. In the Krutenau district of Strasbourg, it's the same story, and in many other areas... 8. Some are mysteriously destroyed by fire... 9. after which the owner builds something else on the site. 'This is too obvious. We must think of something else.' 10. In Strasbourg, the old railway station, the savings bank, the Maison Rouge, etc... 11. Other buildings are left to drug addicts who overdose themselves in them... 'Pay for your fix or I smash your face in!' 'Isn't Amsterdam a tolerant city!' 'Perfect. Six more months and the house will be a ruin and we'll be able to tear it down.' 12. In Strasbourg, the immigrants are in the same situation...slums, abject poverty, etc.... 13. If you want to occupy a house, get in touch with the council first, otherwise you'll be ripped off by the speculators! 14. 'Filthy drug addicts! They've left my building in ruins! Everything will have to come down and be rebuilt!' 'If you were my son I'd give you a good hiding!' 15. Also in Strasbourg the workers are parked on the outskirts of the city in modern estates. The old houses in the city centre are done up and rented or sold to middle-class families at prices that average families can't afford. 16. 'Great, the whole city has been rebuilt. We're waiting for the underground.' 'What's that over there?' 17. 'Oh, that's my home. Pretty isn't it?' 18. 'You'd think we were in Strasbourg.'

Armoederveen eerste episode

Comic by Rob Figee from *Stripje!*, a Dutch political comics magazine, Netherlands, 1974.

Armoederveen (Poverty Borough) — first episode
1. A mysterious figure rifles the files of the Town Hall... 'Hi, hi — hey, what's this? The town is planning to expand...' 2. 'Ah! on the east side of the town! Mmm, tower blocks! Well, well.' 3. A little later 'So, this is where they want to start building...' 4. 'But Poverty Borough will have to pay for it, because I'll be there first! Ha, ha!' 5. 'Well now, my good man, aren't you getting sick to death of your cows? At your age too — you're not looking very well!' 'You think so, sir?' 'Well, now that you say it, sir...' 6. 'I know just the little flat for you! And as you've always worked so hard to feed our hungry countrymen, I'm prepared to offer you a good price for your meadows.' 7. 'BUT, but, but um, I...' (SOLD for f1.20,000.) 'Great! That's settled then — I always come prepared. Look, all you need to do is sign here; a cross will do.' 8. 'And now all I have to do is wait for those chaps from the Town Hall — they've got a surprise coming! Snigger, snigger.'

Pamphlet from Amsterdam harbour, Netherlands, 1972 © BGA.
1. Supplies. Toolkit. 2. Tools. 3. 'Get to work, the ship must leave!'
4. 'You have to learn to live with it.' 5. 'One day this will be my
coffin.' 6. 'Tut, tut, yes, that's life.' 7. 'It's your funeral mates, not
ours!' The fight continues!

Pamphlet from the long wildcat strike in Antwerp harbour,
Belgium, 1973.
1. Union boss and his gang: 'After very difficult and tiring negotiations
we have succeeded in getting our claim accepted by the management: a
great victory for our dockers.' 2. Union boss: 'An increase of 30 francs and
40 francs per shift over two years, approved by our union committees.'
(Monster: Inflation.) 3. Strike on 9/4/73. 'The dockers demand: 100
francs per shift, and a 13th month's pay every year.'

GÉÉN ANGOLA KOFFIE

HET IS EEN KLEINE MOEITE

Pamphlet of successful boycott action against Angolan coffee import
made by Joost Swarte, Netherlands, 1973.

NO ANGOLAN COFFEE

...mmm, a lovely cuppa coffee... Here in Holland we have two kinds of
coffee. Can you taste the difference? Probably not! The greatest
difference lies not in the taste, but in what happens to the money you pay
for it! In three brands (Douwe Egberts, Van Nelle and Niemeyer) Angolan
coffee is used. This coffee is cultivated by forced labour, and the profits
are used by the Portuguese government to wage war against the Angolan
freedom fighters. Many Portuguese boys die every year because they're
forced to fight those Africans. Africans are killed too, and are kicked out
of their villages, their crops are ruined, and without your knowing it,
without your wanting it, you are contributing to this war because you
drink coffee from Angola. But that also means that you can help end that
war. Because if we in Holland refuse to drink any Angolan coffee, that
means an annual 13 million guilders less for that war. It isn't difficult to
switch to a brand that contains no Angolan coffee: the World Store (in
Utrecht) sells coffee from Tanzania — an independent African state, and it
doesn't cost a penny more. Most supermarket chains' own brands likewise
don't contain Angolan coffee. So you see... IT'S A SMALL PRICE TO
PAY but will certainly help!

Robert van der Croft in the *Bajeskrant*, a paper for prison inmates, Netherlands, 1974.

1. 'They must be mad if they think I'm going to *buy* a Christmas tree! Surely there are enough around here?' 2. 'Aha! Caught red-handed!'

3. 'Trespassing…tree chopped down!…that is murder!…yes indeed murder!…with premeditation!…possession of an illegal weapon…vandalism …I sentence you to three months' hard labour!' (exhibit A) 'Oops!'
4. 'Hey you! This ain't no holiday camp! Get on with that chopping!' 'Completely mad!'

MARIËNBURG STRIP

MARIËNBURG

Call for solidarity with Surinam workers in Dutch-run sugar plantation, Netherlands, 1970. © Hetty Paerl.

Mariënburg strip
Exploitation and class struggle on the Mariënburg sugar plantation in Surinam (Dutch Guiana)
Published by the Surinam Committee.

EXPLOITATION

1. In 1882 the Mariënburg sugar plantation was bought by the Dutch Trading Company. Coolies were brought over with false promises from India and later from Java. Hunger and need drove them to leave their country and follow the crimp. Their expectations were betrayed: on one of the first sea voyages from Java to Surinam, 48 of the 612 coolies, squeezed like sardines in the hold, died and 200 became seriously ill. 2. Once arrived at the plantation, conditions turned out to be abominable. Wages and accommodation were totally inadequate. The workers finally revolted: in 1902 a group of 200 attacked and killed the plantation's director. The Dutch army was called in and 17 workers were killed and 39 wounded, of which a further 17 died later. Eight years later this story repeated itself. 3. In 1964 Mariënburg was taken over by the Amsterdam Rubber Company. This company, based in Amsterdam, sucked up the plantation's profits (4.5 million guilders from 1964-8) out of the sweat and misery of the Mariënburg workers and brought it all over to Holland. 4. The field labourers work under the scorching sun. The conditions are atrocious: they have to provide their own tools, they're paid a piece-work rate which means that in order to earn an average wage of 3.50 guilders per day they have to work from 6 a.m. to 6 p.m. Often the whole family has to join in in order to fulfil the daily quota. 5. Conditions in the plant are no better. The refinery, which operates twenty-four hours a day on a three-shift basis, is ancient, dangerous machinery runs everywhere exposed, the workers are not issued with protective helmets or clothing. There are a lot of accidents: a worker who has an accident and loses a limb is bought off with a paltry sum and then fired. 6. Every Saturday the workers have to come and collect their wages even though work stops at 12 o'clock and the law states that staff must be paid during working hours. 1,000 workers have to queue for hours until they are paid. Work continues on public holidays, and if a worker stays away he is not paid. Withholding of pay is a common form of disciplinary action.

WEES SOLIDAIR !
steun het comité « vrienden van mariënburg »

1. As a result of mismanagement, and a decrease in investment, Mariënburg is now on the point of bankruptcy. The management wants to hand its failure over to the workers — after having drained huge profits out of the plantation, in 1972 Amsterdam Rubber threatens to close the place down! This means the livelihood of 1,500 workers and their families — a total of 8,000 people — hangs in the balance. The union organizes strong protest against this threat: 'This plantation was built with the blood and sweat of our forebears. If the place is closed we'll occupy it!' A Committee for the Friends of Mariënburg has been set up to back the workers in their struggle to keep their jobs and raise their living standards. The leaders of the union as well as medical and agricultural experts sit on this committee, whose programme includes the following priorities: (1) Better medical facilities. (2) A public library and a creche for children. (3) A communal agrarian project. 2. As a protection against threatened redundancies and to contribute to a strike fund, the Committee is setting up a communal agrarian project. Bulldozers are levelling the land for the building of pigsties. 3. The pigsties are built by communal effort, and pigs are already installed. 4. The Committee's medical service is free. The waiting room is packed every Sunday with people awaiting treatment and preventive advice. 5. The Committee has also set up a Sunday school to teach children to read and write. Instruction in socialism will come when they have learnt the basic skills. 6. A scout troop has also been set up. Every week the children march through the settlement calling 'Help the aged', 'Help the sick', 'Keep the yard clean'. 7. Surinam and Dutch organizations are supporting the Committee's work with money and technical expertise. Medical equipment, books, money for the acquisition of pigs and a film projector have been sent. The population of Mariënburg can learn about the experience of other people through films, such as Vietnam, Cuba, Angola. Stand by us! Support the Friends of Mariënburg Committee.

GESCHICHTEN VOM DOPPELCHARAKTER

A 'Capital' joke, Germany, 1974. © Verlag für das Studium der Arbeiter-bewegung.
Tales of split personalities.
The first part of *Capital*, drawn and explained by K. Plöckinger and G. Wolfram
1. In the past year prices have risen by 10 per cent — our wages by 3 per cent. We demand our wages to be adjusted! 3. You must be a communist! The devil!